HISTORICAL BACKGROUNDS
OF BIBLE HISTORY

HISTORICAL BACKGROUNDS
OF BIBLE HISTORY

by

Jack P. Lewis

BAKER BOOK HOUSE
Grand Rapids, Michigan

Library of Congress Catalog Card Number 79-156594

ISBN: 0-8010-5507-5

First printing, August 1971
Second printing, June 1973

PHOTOLITHOPRINTED BY CUSHING - MALLOY, INC.
ANN ARBOR, MICHIGAN, UNITED STATES OF AMERICA
1973

THE UNIVERSITY CHRISTIAN STUDENT CENTER
ANNUAL LECTURESHIP

The University Christian Student Center is a private foundation which exists to provide fellowship and guidance in a home away from home atmosphere for university students during their academic careers. While maintaining a dormitory and a fellowship hall adjacent to the university campus, the Center by worship activities, by instruction in Biblical subjects, and by social activities seeks to supplement the classroom educational experiences of the student and to make a contribution toward the enrichment of his life.

As a portion of its regular program, the center sponsors an annual lectureship on "Christian Faith in the Contemporary World" in which a competent Christian lecturer is invited to present a series of lectures on a topic concerning faith that vitally confronts the student during the course of his education. The aim is to present the claims of faith not only as a valid alternative to the secularism which characterizes much of our society, but also as intellectually challenging, and as offering the solution to many of the ills of the current age.

The first in the Christian Center series, lectures by Dr. Jack Wood Sears entitled "Science and the Bible," has experienced a gratifying reception from the public. The book herewith presented, second in the series, represents lectures presented during the winter of 1969.

ACKNOWLEDGMENT

Scripture quotations are from the Revised Standard Version and are used by permission. Material from James B. Pritchard *Ancient Near Eastern Texts Related to the Old Testament* is reprinted by permission of Princeton University Press. Thanks is also extended to Westminster Press for permission to use material from John Bright, *A History of Israel*, copyright by W. L. Jenkins, MCMLIX; to the University of Chicago Press for the use of D. D. Luckenbill, *Ancient Records of Assyria and Babylon*; to the British Museum for D. J. Wiseman, *Chronicles of Chaldean Kings*; to Thomas Nelson and Sons, Ltd, for D. W. Thomas, *Documents from Old Testament Times*; to Harvard University Press for use of the Loeb editions of Josephus and Eusebius; to Oxford University Press for H. Danby, *The Mishna*; to the Society for Promoting Christian Knowledge for C. K. Barrett, *The New Testament Background: Selected Documents*; and to the British School of Archaeology in Iraq for quotations from its publication, *Iraq*.

FOREWORD

Classical Christianity is rooted in history. The early church rejected the teaching that Jesus was not really a man living a real life at a point in history. Luke places the ministry of John the Baptist and the baptism of Jesus at an exact historical moment: "In the fifteenth year of the reign of Tiberias Caesar, Pontius Pilate being governor of Judea, and Herod being tetrarch of Galilee, and his brother Philip tetrarch of the region of Ituraea and Trachonitis, and Lysanias tetrarch of Abilene, in the high-priesthood of Annas and Caiaphas, the word of God came to John the son of Zechariah in the wilderness . . ." (Luke 3:1-2). The church echoed its emphasis on the historical Jesus in the creedal statement that he "suffered under Pontius Pilate."

Docetism, the idea that Jesus seemed to be human but that he did not really have a human body and was not a part of history, has often plagued Old Testament scholars as well as those whose primary concern is with the New Testament. Instead of thinking of real people living in human circumstances, many Christians have chosen to allegorize Biblical history. The attempt to identify Bible characters as types rather than flesh and blood people has made the Bible a book of puzzles to be solved, rather than the revelation of God's words and deeds in history which it claims to be. James (5:17) reminds us, "Elijah was a man of like nature with ourselves. . . ." We do a disservice to ourselves and dishonor the Word of God when we place a gulf between the men of the Bible and ourselves. True, they were removed from us in time, in geography, in language, and in culture. They were, however, men "of like nature with ourselves." Even of Jesus, the Son of God, it was said, that He "increased in wisdom and in stature, and in favor with God and man" (Luke 2:52).

If the Bible is to be taken seriously as a historical document, the serious Bible student must become familiar with the people and events — in and out of Scripture — that had some bearing on the Biblical record. All cannot spend a lifetime in such studies, but all can read authoritative volumes written by competent scholars in the history and archaeology of the Biblical world.

Jack P. Lewis is a scholar who has provided us with a major text dealing in a serious way with Biblical history in the context of Near Eastern History. Dr. Lewis is conservative in the best sense of that term. He is theologically conservative, but he is also cautious, refusing to indulge in speculation where evidence is lacking. A measure of that caution is evident from the fact that the era of Solomon is the first given detailed attention in the book.

Properly used, this book will be an aid to the understanding of the events of the Bible. It is not written to "prove" or to "disprove" the Bible — although its result will be a feeling for the trustworthiness of the Biblical writers. Jack Lewis knows the documents of antiquity and modern literature pertaining to them. He is a cautious and faithful guide, presenting the evidence and trusting the good judgment of his readers to use it properly. Sixty-three persons covering a period of about 1000 years are discussed by the author in some detail. Biblical and archaeological information are skillfully combined to enable the reader to understand what happened — and often why it happened. It is too much to say that God's redemptive revelation in the person of Jesus Christ cannot be known apart from a knowledge of historical backgrounds. It is not too much to say, however, that an understanding of that revelation as it was made in history requires the student of Scripture to attend carefully to the environment in which the events of Scripture took place. The Bible is more than history, as it is more than literature. Just as we miss a proper understanding of Scripture if we fail to recognize its literary forms, so we rob ourselves of the joy of intelligent Bible study if we do not study diligently the people and events of history that relate to the Bible itself. With Jack Lewis as a guide, you will find in this book an excellent introduction to the historical backgrounds of Bible history.

CHARLES F. PFEIFFER

Mt. Pleasant, Michigan
April, 1971

LIST OF ABBREVIATIONS

AASOR	*Annual of American Schools of Oriental Research*
AJA	*American Journal of Archaeology*
AJSL	*American Journal of Semitic Languages and Literature*
ANEP	J. B. Pritchard, *Ancient Near East in Pictures Relating to the Old Testament* (Princeton: Princeton University Press, 1954)
ANET	J. B. Pritchard, ed., *Ancient Near Eastern Texts Related to the Old Testament* (3rd ed.; Princeton: Princeton University Press, 1969)
Ant.	Josephus *Antiquities of the Jews*
ARAB	D. D. Luckenbill, *Ancient Records of Assyria and Babylon* (Chicago: University of Chicago Press, 1926-27), 2 vols.
BA	*Biblical Archaeologist*
BAR	*Biblical Archaeologist Reader*. D. N. Freedman and E. F. Campbell, Jr., eds. (Garden City: Doubleday, 1964)
BASOR	*Bulletin of American Schools of Oriental Research*
BC	K. Lake and F. J. Foakes-Jackson, *Beginnings of Christianity* (London: Macmillan, 1920-1933), 5 vols.
BJRL	*Bulletin of John Rylands Library*
CAH	*Cambridge Ancient History*
C.I.A.	*Corpus Inscriptionum Atticarum*
C.I.G.	*Corpus Inscriptionum Graecarum*
C.I.L.	*Corpus Inscriptionum Latinarum*
C.I.S.	*Corpus Inscriptionum Semiticarum*
CSEL	*Corpus Scriptorum Ecclesiasticorum Latinorum*
G.C.S	*Die griechischen christlichen Schriftsteller der ersten Jahrhunderte*
H.E.	Eusebius *Historia Ecclesiastique*
HTR	*Harvard Theological Review*
IB	*Interpreter's Bible*
IEJ	*Israel Exploration Journal*
ISBE	*International Standard Bible Encyclopaedia*
JBL	*Journal of Biblical Literature*
JCS	*Journal of Cuneiform Studies*
JNES	*Journal of Near Eastern Studies*
JQR	*Jewish Quarterly Review*
JTS	*Journal of Theological Studies*

LCL	*Loeb Classical Library*
LXX	Septuagint
M.	*Mishna*
MV(A)G	*Mitteilungen der vorderasiatisch (-Ägyptisch)er Gesellschaft*
OIP	*Oriental Institute Publications*
PEQ	*Palestine Exploration Quarterly*
PEFQS	*Palestine Exploration Fund Quarterly Statement*
RB	*Revue Biblique*
T.B.	*Babylonian Talmud*
ZAW	*Zeitschrift für die alttestamentliche Wissenschaft*
ZDPV	*Zeitschrift des deutschen Palestina-Vereins*
ZWTH	*Zeitschrift für wissenschaftliche Theologie*

CONTENTS

ILLUSTRATIONS

INTRODUCTION

This study is aimed at the non-specialist rather than at the technical scholar, though it is hoped that the latter will be charitable to its shortcomings. For the benefit of those who may wish to do additional study, references to primary sources and to scholarly treatments are included. The purpose of this investigation is to collect in a convenient summary the materials from archaeological discoveries in which figures identifiable with specific Biblical characters appear. It has not attempted to include the great wealth of material on customs of the relevant periods in which these characters lived — which collection of data ordinarily makes up the body of books on Biblical archaeology. It is in limiting itself to the area of information on characters that this study differs from most available books dealing with Biblical archaeology.

Since, however, these discoveries cannot be evaluated in isolation, the information on Biblical characters from ancient historians — where available — has also been included. It will become obvious that in some of its areas this latter type of information is predominant and archaeological findings are minimal or non-existent. One is cautioned to remember that the information of the historians is not necessarily accurate merely because it is old. In some cases the historians may be only spinning out a concept of Biblical tradition. Finally, since a knowledge of the minutiae of the Bible cannot be assumed on the part of all readers, each section first summarizes the Biblical significance of the character discussed.

The Biblical story is a story involving specific characters who play a part in episodes that took place at specific places and at specific times in history. However, the very nature of the Bible makes the task of this study a difficult one. It is not the purpose of the Bible to tell the history of the Middle East. The Bible is not basically interested in dates or in the social, political, and economic issues that ordinarily make up the substance of history. Its materials are chosen for religious purposes. The early figures at the center of Biblical history were not politically significant and are thereby passed by in silence by the record makers of the Middle East. The nation of Israel is a late-comer on the scene, not really becoming a nation until the end of the second millennium B.C. Previous to this time the ancestors of

Israel came into contact with her neighbors, but foreign figures tend to be anonymous. The pharaohs encountered by Joseph and by Israel during her term of bondage are not designated by their personal names. And so it is with many other Biblical figures. We are at a loss in making specific identifications under these conditions.

Another difficulty facing us is that the information from archaeology is spotty. Other than scattered inscribed potsherds, some ostraca, a few inscribed seals, and sparse inscriptions, the written records of the Hebrew people are entirely in the Bible itself. With few exceptions, the records of Palestinian and Syrian forces with whom Israel struggled have not been found. For the Old Testament period information is therefore limited to Egyptian, Assyrian, Babylonian, and Persian records. Thus, the incompleted task of archaeology makes a study of this type provisional.

A number of cautions are in order. The interest in collecting external material on Biblical characters is at least as old as the first century when Josephus issued his *Antiquities of the Jews*. The history of this type of undertaking vividly illustrates the major danger in such activity — identifications made on insufficient evidence. Justin Martyr, in the second century, claimed to have found in Rome evidence that Simon Magus was worshipped there. The evidence was an inscription to the Sabine god, *Simoni Sancto*. The false identification is repeated uncritically by a host of later church writers. Eusebius compiled his own list of false identifications — including the one just mentioned — by overlooking chronological and other difficulties that stood in the way. Recent Biblical archaeology has not been free of this sort of activity, and more than one identification has, upon fuller investigation, had to be abandoned. To cite only one example, Amraphel king of Shinar, at one time identified with Hammurabi, is now known to have antedated him by several centuries and it is now universally admitted that we do not have information on any of the figures of Genesis fourteen. Archaeological conclusions — like conclusions in other areas — are subject to continual re-evaluation. It is entirely possible that some identifications now championed will later be abandoned.

As a further word of caution, this type of study has built into it the hazard of an unintentional invitation to the reader to conclude more than the investigation accomplishes. Establishing that there is historical evidence for the existence of a figure and establishing the veracity of a particular episode in his career are two separate steps. This study is aimed more at doing the former than the latter. It is only for a small minority of these figures with which we deal that we have archaeological material on the specific episode mentioned in the Bible. In most cases our information supplements that given in the Bible.

While scholars never tire of heaping coals on the head of the overeager apologist, perhaps his fault is not more serious than that of the unduly skeptical scholar whose bias prompts him to ignore or to misinterpret certain pertinent data. The very nature of the case makes it likely that there always will be more Biblical characters known only from the Bible than there are about whom we have archaeological information. Adam, Noah, Abraham, Isaac, Jacob, Moses, Joshua, Samuel, Saul, David, Solomon, Elijah, Elisha, and all the writing prophets — to mention only a few figures — all fall into this category. Claims of discoveries of Biblical figures earlier than the time of Solomon have upon fuller investigation repeatedly been found to be without foundation. At the same time there is a growing body of material on Biblical characters in the periods later than the division of the Israelite kingdom. The existence of characters like Sargon and Belshazzar has been established, and the careers of others have been illuminated and supplemented. Archaeological study has both solved some problems and has brought to light other unresolved problems for Biblical study. Such problems where relevant have not been passed over in complete silence. On the one hand, it is hoped that the study has succeeded in avoiding the pitfall of claiming more for the material than candid scholarship can admit, and, on the other hand, of neglecting to bring to light facts that should be readily available to the man who is interested.

Not at all a new discovery, this study is a compilation. Its heavy borrowing from the labors of others — which indebtedness is hereby acknowledged — will be obvious to all oriented in the field. A quick check of the dictionaries and archaeological handbooks will reveal how that over the past century and a half this information has been coming to light. A brief, earlier listing of the majority of the characters is to be found in R. D. Wilson, *A Scientific Investigation of the Old Testament*, revised by E. J. Young (Chicago: Moody Press, 1959), pp. 64-75. The study does have an item or two borrowed from journal articles that have not yet had time to be absorbed into the handbooks. If there is any originality at all, it is in compilation and summarization.

I

FROM SHISHAK TO HOPHRA

The scholar who sets himself to attempt a synthesis between archaeological materials and Biblical materials dealing with specific Egyptian characters immediately experiences two frustrations. First, while in the early period a sizeable number of pharaohs and some Egyptian private figures are known to have had contact with Palestine, none of these figures before the time of the divided kingdom are mentioned in the Bible by name and none of the episodes in which they are involved are surveyed in the Bible. Second, other than a few more or less private figures, who, like most private men in any generation, are destined to live out their lives and then sink back into silent dust, Egyptians who do appear in early portions of the Bible are anonymous figures.

EGYPTIANS IN PALESTINE

It is conjectured that the campaign of Pepi I (*ca.* 2350 B.C.) to the "land of the Sand-Dwellers," spoken of in an inscription found in the tomb of Uni, his commander, was a campaign against Palestine. The forces proceeded by land and sea and claimed complete victory after cutting down "fig trees and vines" and throwing down enclosures. The army proceeded as far as "Antelope-nose," supposed to be the Carmel range of mountains.[1] At a later time the Execration Texts of the twentieth and nineteenth centuries B.C. preserved Palestinian place names like Askelon, Jerusalem, and Hazor, and also names of some rulers, but none of the rulers are Biblical figures.[2]

---

1 *ANET*, pp. 227-228.
2 Y. Aharoni and M. Avi-Yonah, *The Macmillan Bible Atlas* (New York: Macmillan, 1968), No. 23.

13

Sinuhe, fleeing from the wrath of Pharaoh, spent his period of exile in the Palestinian area about 1960-1921 B.C. and left a description of the land:

> It was a good land, named Yaa. Figs were in it, and grapes. It had more wine than water. Plentiful was its honey, abundant its olives. Every (kind of) fruit was on its trees. Barley was there, and emmer. There was no limit to any (kind of) cattle. Moreover, great was that which accrued to me as a result of the love of me. He made me ruler of a tribe of the choicest of his country. Bread was made for me as daily fare, wine as daily provision, cooked meat and roast fowl, beside the wild beasts of the desert, for they hunted for me and laid before me, beside the catch of my own hounds. Many . . . were made for me, and milk in every (kind of) cooking.[3]

The chief of the Semites, a people who had come to Egypt to trade and who were depicted in the Beni Hasan tombs about 1892 B.C., was Ibsha.[4] Later, Semites, known as the Hyksos rulers of Egypt, were expelled by Ahmoses I around 1570 B.C., but none of these figures mentioned are Biblical figures.

Thutmose III fought against and overcame Canaanite forces in an attack on Megiddo in 1468 B.C. Thutmose left behind in a relief on the temple of Amon at Karnack a description of this campaign which is one of the earliest accounts of military tactics on record.[5] A portion of a stele, probably of Thutmose, has been found at Tell el-'Oreimeh on the shores of Galilee.[6] Amenhotep II carried out campaigns in 1431 and in 1429 B.C.[7] The Amarna letters are correspondence from Palestinian figures during the reigns of Amenhotep III and Amenhotep IV (Akhenaton).[8] These letters preserve both numerous place names and personal names. Still later Seti I carried out a campaign in the area of Bethshan about 1303 B.C. and a stele of his has been found at the excavation of that site.[9] Ramses II fought at Kadesh on the Orontes in 1285 B.C. and a treaty with the Hittites was

---

3 *ANET*, pp. 18-22, Nos. 80-90.
4 J. Finegan, *Light From the Ancient Past* (Princeton: Princeton University Press, 1959), pp. 92-93.
5 Aharoni and Avi-Yonah, *op. cit.*, Nos. 32-34; *ANET*, pp. 234-238.
6 C. C. McCowan, *The Ladder of Progress in Palestine* (New York: Harper and Bros., 1943), p. 164.
7 Aharoni and Avi-Yonah, *op. cit.*, Nos. 35-36; *ANET*, pp. 245-247.
8 *ANET*, pp. 483 ff.
9 *Ibid.*, pp. 253-254.

concluded giving Egypt southern Syria and Palestine.[10] A monument of his has also been found at Bethshan.[11] Within the citadel at Joppa were discovered in 1955-1958 portals of the city gates inscribed with fragments of the titles and names of Ramses II.[12] Merneptah in 1220 B.C. was victorious in Canaan and set up a monument which was found by Petrie at Thebes on which he claimed:

> Plundered is the Canaan with every evil;
> Carried off is Askelon; seized upon is Gezer;
> Yanoam is made as that which does not exist;
> Israel is laid waste, his seed is not.[13]

This is the one and only known specific mention of Israel on an Egyptian monument.

Ramses III (1195-1164 B.C.), who defeated the sea peoples and recorded his victory in the temple of Amon at Medinet Habu, also left at Bethshan a statue and a door lintel with an inscription of one of his officials.[14] Wen-Amon traveled to Dor and to Byblos in the early eleventh century to acquire wood for a ceremonial barge for the god Amon.[15]

Of course, some of these names of Egyptians loom large in conjectural synchronisms with Biblical history, but alas! none of these characters and none of these matters in which they are involved come within the scope of purpose of the Biblical writers.

EGYPTIANS IN THE BIBLE

Already in Genesis the Bible reader encounters in Egypt the names of Potiphar, the captain of the Egyptian guard (Gen. 39:1); Asenath who became the wife of Joseph; Potiphera the priest of On, father of Asenath (Gen. 41:45); and Hagar, the Egyptian concubine of Abraham (Gen. 16:1). Scattered Israelites have names of Egyptian derivation. Such were Moses and Aaron's grandson, Phinehas (Num. 25:6-13; 31:6; cf. Ps. 106: 30-31; Josh. 22:13, 30-34; Judg. 20:28), in the period of the Exodus. Even as late as the period of the Judges names of others

---

10 *Ibid.*, pp. 201-203.
11 *Ibid.*, p. 255.
12 J. Kaplan, "The Fifth Season of the Excavation at Joffa," *JQR*, n.s., LIV (Oct., 1963), 110.
13 *ANET*, p. 378.
14 G. E. Wright, "The Discoveries at Megiddo 1935-1939," *BA*, XIII (1950), 36.
15 *ANET*, pp. 25-29.

like Hophni and Phinehas, sons of Eli (I Sam. 2:34), are of like derivation.[16] Up to this time sources outside the Bible have nothing to say of any of these personages. Their significance is in salvation history and not in the social, political, and economic areas where the records of time ordinarily are preserved.

Other Egyptian figures, however, are designated only by their titles: Pharaoh, the Chief Butler, and the Chief Baker. Abram came to Egypt in a time of famine (Gen. 12:10-20), but the particular pharaoh with whom he dealt is not distinguished from the many other figures of the same title who held office. So it is also with the pharaoh whose dream Joseph interpreted and who exalted Joseph to rule over Egypt (Gen. 41). Neither is the "king who knew not Joseph," who oppressed the Israelites, but who died while Moses was in Midian, further distinguished (Exod. 1-2). Pharaoh's daughter, who had pity upon the babe in the river, who gave him his name, and who reared Moses, is an unnamed personage (Exod. 2:3-10). The pharaoh in whose presence Moses and Aaron stood as they brought on the ten plagues and who lost his firstborn in the last of the plagues is only designated as pharaoh.

By a series of chronological conjectures those who champion the early date of the Exodus equate the pharaohs concerned with known figures from Egyptian history that fit their chronology such as Thutmose III (1490-1436 B.C.) and Amenhotep II (1436-1410 B.C.). By a different series of conjectures those who favor the late date and those who popularize the late date by movies and books based on that date, propose names that fit into the chronological framework they have adopted. Here the names of Seti I (ca. 1302-1290 B.C.) and Ramses II (1290-1224 B.C.) loom large.

But when all the logic has been used and all the propaganda has been set forth, despite general consensus at various times, the seekers for certainty, one and all, are doomed to perpetual frustration. Despite our wishes the Biblical writers for the early period supplied us with no names upon which identifications can be made.

Solomon took as a wife pharaoh's daughter whose father then proceeded to capture Gezer, to destroy it, and to present it to his daughter as a dowry (I Kings 3:1; 9:16, 24). It is assumed that the pharaohs of the twenty-first dynasty are contemporaneous with Solomon and a recent case argues that Siamon is the

---

16 M. Noth, *Die israelitischen Personennamen im Rahmen der gemein-semitischen Namengebung* (Stuttgart: W. Kohlhammer, 1928), p. 63.

most likely candidate.[17] In the later years of Solomon's reign, Hadad the Edomite was received into Egypt favorably and received in marriage from pharaoh the sister of Tahpenes the queen of Egypt (I Kings 11:14-22). The name of this queen has not been identified in hieroglyphics.[18]

SHISHAK

The first Egyptian figure mentioned by name in the Bible about which we have information from sources other than Josephus is Shishak. Earlier Jeroboam had been appointed by Solomon to be in charge of forced labor of the people of Joseph in Solomon's building projects. He had been designated by the prophet Ahijah with a symbolic tearing of the garment to receive ten portions of the kingdom over which he would rule. After plotting against Solomon, Jeroboam fled for his life to Egypt and there found refuge with Shishak until the death of Solomon at which time he returned to be an opponent of Rehoboam (I Kings 11:26-40; cf. II Chron. 10:2 and I Kings 12:20).

1. GOLDEN BRACELETS made for Nemareti, son of the Egyptian Pharaoh Shishak I (c. I Kings 14:25). Courtesy, British Museum

In the fifth year of the reign of Rehoboam, son of Solomon, Shishak in an effort to restore the former glories of Egypt led an army of Egyptians, Libyans, and Ethiopians into Palestine, took the fortified cities of Judah as far as Jerusalem and from there took away the treasures of the house of the Lord, the treasures of the king's house, and the shields of gold that Solomon had made. This tribute paid by the king saved the city of

---

17 See the conjecture of S. H. Horn, "Who Was Solomon's Egyptian Father-in-Law?" *Biblical Research*, XII (1967), 3-17.

18 A. Gardiner, *Egypt of the Pharaohs* (Oxford: Clarendon Press, 1961), p. 329.

Jerusalem. The gold shields were then replaced by Rehoboam with brass shields (I Kings 14:25-28; II Chron. 12:1-12).

Shishak is to be identified with Sheshonk I, the Egyptian founder of the Twenty-second Dynasty to whom Manetho attributes a reign of twenty-one years,[19] and whose reign is dated by Albright as 935-914 B.C. The campaign in Palestine is dated at 918 B.C.[20] Sheshonk, upon the completion of his Palestinian campaign mentioned above, erected a relief victory monument at the south entrance (the Bubastite portal) of the temple of his god Amon in Karnak. Unfortunately the specific regnal year of the campaign is not given and unfortunately also there is no narrative account. The monument — with a list of more than 150 conquered cities — would indicate that Shishak's campaign was considerably more extensive than one would conjecture from Scripture, which gives neither the line of march nor the cities attacked. In the list from the monument, towns of Judah, Israel, and Edom are included, extending as far north as Bethshan and perhaps as far south as Ezion Geber (cf. town 73/4) where the excavator found a destruction layer which he attributed to this campaign.[21]

About a dozen northern cities have been identified from the king's list at Karnak. Well known along the line of march are Gaza, Gezer, Ayalon, Gibeon, Sukkoth, Bethshan, Taanach, and Megiddo. It is interesting to observe that excavators of some of these towns have also found destruction layers from this period which they attribute to Shishak's attacks. It would seem that the army returned south along the Via Maris. A second part of the list deals with Negeb sites and includes Arad.[22] The campaign of Shishak in Palestine was not followed up. The successors of Shishak were not able to exploit any advantage the campaign could have afforded them.[23]

---

19 Manetho, Aegyptiaca (Epitome), trans. W. G. Waddell (LCL, Cambridge: Harvard University Press, 1956), p. 159.

20 W. F. Albright, The Excavation of Tell Beit Mirsim (Annual of American Schools of Oriental Research, Vol. XXI; New Haven: American Schools of Oriental Research, 1941), III, 37. Gardiner, op. cit., p. 329, suggests a date of 930 B.C.

21 Nelson Glueck, "Ezion-geber," BA, XXVIII (1965), 82; "The Second Campaign at Tell El-Kheleifeh (Ezion-geber: Elath)," BASOR, No. 75 (1939), 17 ff.

22 B. Mazar, "The Campaign of Pharaoh Shishak to Palestine," Supplements to Vetus Testamentum, IV (1957), 57-66; D. M. Noth, "Die Schoshenkliste," ZDPV, LXI (1938), 277-304.

23 W. F. Albright, "New Light from Egypt on the Chronology and History of Israel and Judah," BASOR, No. 130 (April, 1953), 4-8.

2. WALL OF THE TEMPLE AT KARNAK, Egypt, with inscription commemorating Shishak's victory over Rehoboam of Judah. Courtesy, Matson Photo Service

Though it has also been conjectured that this was the pharaoh whose daughter Solomon married (I Kings 3:1), and who gave Gezer to his daughter as a present (I Kings 9:16),[24] it is unlikely that Jeroboam could have found safety at a court so favorable to Solomon. A more recent conjecture, as suggested above, would nominate Siamon of the Twenty-first Dynasty for Solomon's father-in-law.[25]

A fragment of a victory stele of Shishak set up in Megiddo has been found in the rubbish heap of Schumacher's excavation of that site.[26] Also a chair of a seated statue found at Byblos bears Shishak's name. It is conjectured that this statue may have been a gift of the king.[27]

In 1938-1939 the intact burial chamber of Sheshonk I was reported discovered at Tanis by Montet. The body of the king was splendidly arrayed, with a gold mask over his face, and enclosed in a coffin of electrum.[28] More recently Montet revokes the previous identification and states that the resting place of Sheshonk I remains an enigma. The tomb found seems to be that of a previously unknown Sheshonk whose chronological position is uncertain. Only some cartouches of Sheshonk I and a few other objects from his time have been identified from the tomb of Psusennes at Tanis.[29]

So, King of Egypt

Hoshea, the last king of Israel, had been put on the throne with the approval of Tiglath-pileser of Assyria. Following the death of Tiglath-pileser he took advantage of the opportunity to plot revolt in an effort to gain his freedom from his overlord. Shalmaneser V found treachery in him in that "he sent messengers to So, king of Egypt, and offered no tribute to the king of

---

24 J. H. Breasted, *A History of Egypt* (2d ed.; New York: Scribner's, 1909), p. 529; W. O. E. Oesterley, "Egypt and Israel," *The Legacy of Egypt*, ed. S. R. K. Glanville (Oxford: University Press, 1942), pp. 225-226; A. Alt, "Israel und Aegypten," *Beiträge zur Wissenschaft vom Alten Testament*, VI (1909), 19 ff.; A. T. Olmstead, *History of Palestine and Syria* (New York: Scribner's, 1931; reprinted 1965), p. 340.

25 Horn, *op. cit.*, pp. 3-17.

26 R. S. Lamon and G. M. Shipton, *Megiddo* (Oriental Institute Publications, Vol. XLII; Chicago: Chicago University Press, 1939), I, 60-61.

27 R. Dussaud, "Les Inscriptions Pheniciennes du tombeau d'Ahiram, roi de Byblos," *Syria*, V (1924), 145-147.

28 W. S. Smith, "News Items from Egypt: The Seasons of 1938 to 1939 in Egypt," *AJA*, XLIV (1940), 145; Finegan, *op. cit.*, p. 126.

29 Pierre Montet, *Lives of the Pharaohs* (Cleveland and New York: World Publishing Company, 1968), pp. 232-242.

Assyria, as he had done year by year" (II Kings 17:4). This intrigue on the part of Hoshea brought a prompt end to his freedom and brought the final downfall of Israel. Shalmaneser besieged Samaria, it fell, and its people were exiled in 722 B.C.

So, king of Egypt, is one of the most problematic figures of Old Testament history. Josephus at this point merely repeats Biblical information.[30] Despite the fact that one is called king and the other commander in chief, Peet and many others have conjectured that So is the Sib'e, the commander in chief (*turtan*) of Musri, mentioned in Sargon's annals for the year 720 B.C.[31] as an ally of Hanno, King of Gaza.[32] H. Winckler, much earlier, argued that country in Sargon's annals was not Egypt at all, but was the north Arabian kingdom of *Musri*.[33] Winckler has failed to convince most modern scholars, and the identity of So has remained in doubt. Bright remarked: "The So (*Sib'e*) whom Hoshea approached was king, if king he was, only of a part of the Nile Delta. . . . He may have been only an officer of one of the rival rulers of Egypt."[34]

Other efforts have attempted to identify So with either Shabaka or Shabataka of the Twenty-fifth Egyptian Dynasty,[35] but this effort has been rejected by Steindorff on philological and chronological grounds.[36] Yeivin has argued that So is not a personal name, but is a title of "the vizier of the king of Egypt" who was resident in Lower Egypt.[37]

The most recent contribution to this question has been the re-examination of the Sargonic text by R. Borger, who argues that the correct reading of the name is *Re'e* and not *Sib'e*.[38] H. Goedicke then proceeded to argue that So of the Bible is in reality the Hebrew form of the Egyptian place name "Sais" and not a personal name at all. He suggested that Tefnakhte who

---

30 *Ant.* ix. 14. 1 (277).

31 *ANET*, p. 285.

32 T. E. Peet, *Egypt and the Old Testament* (Liverpool: University Press, 1922), pp. 170-171.

33 H. Winckler, "Musri, Meluhha, Maᶜin," *MV(Ä)G*, III (1898), 1 ff.

34 J. Bright, *A History of Israel* (Philadelphia: Westminster, 1959), p. 258.

35 F. Petrie, *Egypt and Israel* (London: S.P.C.K., 1912), pp. 75-77.

36 G. Steindorff, "Die keilschriftliche Wiedergabe ägyptischer Eigennamen," *Beiträge zur Assyriologie*, I (1890), 340 f.

37 S. Yeivin, "Who was 'So' the King of Egypt?" *Vetus Testamentum*, II (1952), 164-168.

38 "Das Ende des ägyptischen Feldherrn Sib'e = נסא ," *JNES*, XIX (1960), 49 ff.

resided in Sais would have been a potential ally for Hoshea.[39] Albright, proposing that the preposition "'el" ("unto") has fallen out of the text by haplography, suggested a reading "to Sais, to the king of Egypt," and listed Goedicke's suggestion "among the most important clarifications of Biblical history in recent years."[40]

It is not likely that So will so graciously die without additional struggle. The new explanation — right or wrong — goes in the face of the entire exegetical tradition which began at least as early as the Septuagint version (ca. 250 B.C.) which took So as a person and spelled his name *Segar* with the variant spelling *Soa*.

Tirhakah

During Sennacherib's invasion of Palestine in 701 B.C., the Rabshakeh returned from Jerusalem, where he had confronted the representatives of Hezekiah. He found the king of Assyria no longer fighting against Lachish, but now fighting against Libnah. There Sennacherib heard rumors that Tirhakah, king of Ethiopia, had set out to fight against him. He again sent messengers to Hezekiah to make further demands of him (II Kings 19:9; Isa. 37:9). Egypt had proved to be "that broken reed of a staff" which the Rabshakeh had suggested that she would be (Isa. 36:6; II Kings 18:21; cf. Ezek. 29:6-7).

Tirhakah was a king of Ethiopia and of Egypt (689-664 B.C.) in the Twenty-fifth Dynasty, which dynasty included at least the three kings: Shabaka, Shabataka, and Taharqa.[41] He was third successor to his father Piankhi who had conquered and unified Egypt to establish the Twenty-fifth Dynasty. Piankhi withdrew from Egypt but his brother Shabaka subdued it anew and killed the pharaoh to establish himself.

Tirhakah is known from both Egyptian and Assyrian sources. In Egypt there is a funeral stele of an Apis bull said to have been born in the twenty-sixth year of Tirhakah.[42] Also the University of Oxford excavation (1930-1931) at Kawa in Nubia has turned up five steles of Tirhakah which in part parallel records

---

39 "The End of 'So, King of Egypt,'" *BASOR*, No. 171 (Oct., 1963), 64-66.

40 W. F. Albright, "The Elimination of King 'So'," *BASOR*, No. 171 (Oct., 1963), 66.

41 Cf. Manetho, *op. cit.*, p. 167.

42 J. M. A. Janssen, "Que sait-on actuellement du Pharaon Taharqa?" *RB*, XXXIV (1953), 26; J. H. Breasted, *Ancient Records of Egypt* (New York: Russell & Russell, 1906; reprinted 1962), IV, No. 962.

known from other sites.[43] There is also a long mutilated inscription of his in a temple he built at Sanam.[44] He did building at Karnak, where he is depicted in worship, and at Medinet Habu.[45] One of the figures of the Senjirli stele, where Esarhaddon has two captive kings on leashes, is Tirhakah. His negroid features can be seen.[46] A number of art objects are also marked with his name.[47] His rifled tomb was found near Napata by G. Reisner; however, Reisner failed to publish his findings.[48]

Tirhakah is also frequently met in Assyrian records, though those that specify his name deal with events later than the Biblical episode. Sennacherib, in the Oriental Institute prism, without giving their names, speaks of Hezekiah's dependence upon the kings of Egypt and the king of Ethiopia. He claims to have defeated them in the plain of Eltekeh.[49]

Tirhakah later attempted to defend Egypt against the advances of Esarhaddon and Ashurbanipal, but was driven from the Delta into Upper Egypt where he maintained himself at Thebes. Both of these Assyrians mention their struggles against him. Esarhaddon reports:

> I conquered Tyre which is (an island) amidst the sea. I took away all the towns and the possessions of Ba'lu its king, who had put his trust on Tirhakah (Tarqû), king of Nubia (Kûsu). I conquered Egypt (Muṣur), Paturi[si] and Nubia. Its king, Tirhakah, I wounded five times with arrowshots and ruled over his entire country; I car[ried much booty away].[50]

In an account of his campaign of his tenth year, Esarhaddon reports:

> In the course of my campaign I threw up earthwork (for a siege) against Ba'lu king of Tyre who had put his trust upon his friend Tirhakah (Tarqû), king of Nubia (Kûsu), and (therefore) had thrown off the yoke of Ashur, my lord; answering (my admonitions with) insolence.[51]

Esarhaddon also summarized his victory over Tirhakah whom he mentions by name and whom he calls "the one accursed by

43 Janssen, op. cit., p. 26.
44 Ibid., p. 35.
45 Gardiner, op. cit., pp. 345, 348.
46 ANET, p. 293; ANEP, pp. 154, 300-301, No. 447.
47 ANEP, No. 424 and see bibliography in Janssen, op. cit., p. 35, n. 3.
48 See Janssen, op. cit., p. 39, n. 1.
49 ANET, p. 287.
50 Ibid., p. 290.
51 Ibid., p. 292.

all the great gods" on the Senjirli stele[52] and on the Dog River stele.[53] The Esarhaddon chronicle relates how that in the first year of Shamashshumukin the army of Assyria marched against Tirhakah (*Tarqû*) king of Egypt.[54] Ashurbanipal, successor to Esarhaddon, also lists Tirhakah among those against whom he struggled:

> In my first campaign I marched against Egypt (*Magon*) and Ethiopia (*Meluhha*). Tirhakah (*Tarqû*), king of Egypt (*Mu-ṣur*) and Nubia (*Kûsu*), whom Esarhaddon, king of Assyria, my father, had defeated and in whose country he (Esarhaddon) had ruled, this (same) Tirhakah forgot the might of Assur, Ishtar, and the (other) great gods, my lords, and put his trust upon his own power.[55]

Ashurbanipal also summarizes other conflicts with Tirhakah.

The currently accepted chronology for the Twenty-fifth Egyptian Dynasty is premised on the hypothesis proposed by M. F. Laming Macadam which assigned a birthdate of 709 B.C. to Tirhakah and also assigned him a co-regency of six years with Shabataka. Leclant and Yoyotte have challenged the correctness of the interpretation of the data upon which Macadam rested his claim of a co-regency and also have proposed that Shabataka may have ascended the throne as early as 701 B.C. At this stage of knowledge there are some uncertainties connected with both the accession date of Shabataka and with the length of his reign. According to the Kawa stele Tirhakah left his mother and came to Egypt in his twentieth year to be associated with Shabataka, but no text is explicit on what year of Shabataka that was. Macadam assumed that it was 689 B.C., the beginning of his assumed co-regency, but if it should prove to be 701 B.C., or earlier, then instead of being a mere lad at the time of Sennacherib's invasion, Tirhakah would have been twenty or more and would have been old enough to lead an army.[56]

Nevertheless, most scholarship has proceeded on the chronology proposed by Macadam and has attempted to offer hypotheses

---

52 *Ibid.*, p. 293.
53 *Ibid.*
54 *Ibid.*, p. 303.
55 *Ibid.*, p. 294.
56 M. F. L. Macadam, *Temples of Kawa: Oxford University Excavations in Nubia* (Oxford: Oxford University Press, 1949), I, 18 ff.; J. Leclant and J. Yoyotte, "Notes d'histoire et de civilisation ethiopiennes. A propos d'un ouvrage recent," *Bulletin de l'Institut francais d'Archeologie Orientale*, LI (1952), 24-27; R. K. Harrison, *Introduction to the Old Testament* (Grand Rapids: Eerdmans, 1969), pp. 190-191.

to alleviate chronological problems. One effort proposes that ←—
the name of Tirhakah has been substituted in the Biblical texts
for the name of his predecessor. A second assumes that Tirhakah, rather than actually being king at the time of the siege
of Jerusalem, was acting as general for his uncle Shabaka and
that in the Biblical record he is called king proleptically.[57]
However, the current opinions of the date of Tirhakah's birth
would make this assumption completely impossible, as has been
stated above. A third proposal assumes that an episode from
the activities of Esarhaddon, ca. 675 B.C., has been transposed
to the careers of Hezekiah and Sennacherib.[58] Yet a fourth effort conjectures that Sennacherib carried on a second campaign
in the West as late as 688 B.C. at which time he dealt with
Tirhakah and rebellious Hezekiah and that at this time his army
was smitten before Pelusium.[59] Assyrian sources are silent about
such a campaign. This conjecture assumes that Biblical writers did not make clear a distinction between the two campaigns
of Sennacherib which are separated by at least fifteen years. It
has long been recognized that in this same context Sennacherib's
assassination is recounted without indication of lapse of time
despite the fact that it occurred twenty years after 701 B.C. If
there is to be inserted a lapse of time between the siege of
Jerusalem (701 B.C.) and the destruction of Sennacherib's army
(making it to be as late as 688 B.C.) as the fourth alternative
proposes, there would not be an additional need to assume another unmentioned extended time between the destruction of
the army and Sennacherib's death which came in 681 B.C. The
destruction of the army and the murder of Sennacherib are related in the Bible without indication of lapse of time (II
Kings 19:35-37).

Pharaoh Necho

Following the fall of Nineveh in 612 B.C., Assyria was aided ←—
in its dying struggles by Necho who doubtlessly had no desire
to see Babylon move into the vacuum left by the demise of Assyria. His predecessor, Psammetichus I, had been able to invade
Philistia and to besiege Ashdod. According to Herodotus, Psammetichus had at the very border of Egypt bought off the Scythians, who had swept out of the Caucasus through Asia, and only

---

57 Breasted, op. cit., p. 455.
58 Sidney Smith, "Sennacherib and Esarhaddon," CAH, III, 74, 85.
59 Cf. Herodotus Histories ii. 141.

thereby had saved his realm.[60] To Necho time now seemed right for a revival of Egyptian territorial aims. He began his expansion with the seizure of Gaza and Askelon, but Jeremiah threatened of the rising danger out of the north (Jer. 47:1-7). In another undated oracle Jeremiah threatens an invasion of Egypt by Nebuchadnezzar. Pharaoh is the "noisy one who lets the hour go by" (Jer. 46:17).

As Necho went up to the Euphrates to aid Ashuruballit, king of Assyria, Josiah opposed him at Megiddo and was slain for his trouble (II Kings 23:29). The book of Chronicles reports the confrontation as follows:

> After all this, when Josiah had prepared the temple, Neco king of Egypt went up to fight at Carchemish on the Euphrates and Josiah went out against him. . . . Nevertheless Josiah would not turn away from him, but disguised himself in order to fight with him. He did not listen to the words of Neco from the mouth of God, but joined battle in the plain of Megiddo. And the archers shot King Josiah; and the king said to his servants, "Take me away, for I am badly wounded" (II Chron. 35:20, 22-23).

Of this battle Herodotus reports:

> He [Necho] used these ships at need, and with his land army met and defeated the Syrians at Magdolus, taking the great Syrian city of Cadytis after the battle. He sent to Branchidea of Miletus and dedicated there to Apollo the garments in which he won these victories.[61]

In the absence of a major confrontation at the Euphrates at this time (609 B.C.), Necho drew back to Riblah on the Orontes to which he summoned Jehoahaz whom the people had chosen to replace Josiah, clamped him in irons, and took him to Egypt where Jehoahaz died. Necho levied a tribute of 100 talents of silver and a talent of gold on Judah. He proceeded to make another son of Josiah — Eliakim — to be king and changed his name to Jehoiakim (II Kings 23:31-35; II Chron. 36:1-4).

Eventually Babylon was ready to deal with the problem, and Nabopolassar dispatched his son Nebuchadnezzar to oppose Necho. The armies met at Carchemish on the Euphrates in 605 B.C. Jeremiah gives an oracle which is headed:

---

60 *Ibid.*, i. 105.
61 *Ibid.*, ii. 159.

> Concerning the army of Pharaoh Neco, king of Egypt, which was by the river Euphrates at Carchemish and which Nebuchadrezzar king of Babylon defeated in the fourth year of Jehoiakim the son of Josiah, king of Judah (Jer. 46:2).

According to the prophet, "The Lord God of hosts holds a sacrifice in the north country by the river Euphrates" (Jer. 46:10). The Egyptians were routed and retreated to the Delta; their territorial hopes had vanished. The writer of the book of Kings tersely reports:

> And the king of Egypt did not come again out of his land, for the king of Babylon had taken all that belonged to the king of Egypt and from the Brook of Egypt to the river Euphrates (II Kings 24:7).

Both Josephus and the Babylonian Chronicle survey Egyptian-Babylonian clashes of this period. Josephus remarks that Necho "marched . . . to make war on the Medes and the Babylonians who had overthrown the power of the Assyrian empire."[62] The Babylonian Chronicle does not give the name of the pharaoh, but does describe the Egyptian advance in 609 B.C.:

> In the month of Tammuz, Ashur-uballet, king of Assyria, a great Egyptian army crossed the river . . . marched against the city of Harran to conquer it. . . . The garrison which the king of Akkad had stationed in it they . . . slew . . . and he encamped against the city of Harran, until the month of Elul he made an attack upon the city and took nothing, but did not withdraw.[63]

At Sidon were found portions of a stele from this period of Egyptian supremacy in Syria with Necho's name in hieroglyphic.[64]

The continuing struggle for control of Syria by Egypt resulting in the clash at Carchemish, is also reported by both Josephus and by the Babylonian Chronicle. The former says:

---

62 *Ant.* x. 5. 1 (74).

63 D. J. Wiseman, *Chronicles of Chaldean Kings* (London: British Museum, 1956), p. 63.

64 F. L. Griffith, "The God Set of Ramessu II and an Egypto-Syrian Deity," *Proceedings of the Society of Biblical Archaeology*, XVI (Jan. 9, 1894), 90-91; B. Porter and R. L. B. Moss, *Topographical Bibliography of Ancient Egyptian Hieroglyphic Texts, Reliefs, and Paintings* (Oxford: Clarendon Press, 1951), VII, 384.

In the fourth year of his reign someone called Nebuchadnezzar became ruler of the Babylonians and at the same time went up with a great armament against the city of Karchamissa — this is on the Euphrates river — with the determination to make war on the Egyptian king Nechaō, to whom all Syria was subject. When Nechaō learned of the Babylonian king's purpose and of the expedition against him, he himself did not show indifference but set out for the Euphrates with a large force to oppose Nebuchadnezzar. In the engagement that took place he was defeated and lost many myriads in the battle. Then the Babylonian king crossed the Euphrates and occupied all Syria, with the exception of Judaea, as far as Pelusium.[65]

The Babylonian Chronicle without mentioning that Necho was present describes the clash:

Nebuchadnezzar his eldest son, the crown prince, mustered (the Babylonian army) and took command of his troops; he marched to Carchemish which is on the banks of the Euphrates, and crossed the river (to go) against the Egyptian army which lay in Carchemish, . . . fought with each other and the Egyptian army withdrew before him. He accomplished their defeat and to non-existence [beat?] them. As for the rest of the Egyptian army which had escaped from the defeat (so quickly that) no weapon had reached them, in the district of Hamath the Babylonian troops overtook and defeated them so that not a single man [escaped] to his own country. At that time Nebuchadnezzar conquered the whole area of the Hatti-country.[66]

→   It was Necho II (609-595 B.C.), a pharaoh of the Twenty-sixth Dynasty, who is involved in these episodes. While Necho I, king of Memphis and Sais, is mentioned several times by Ashurbanipal,[67] Necho II was not mentioned by name either on Babylonian or Assyrian monuments.[68] Neither do Egyptian sources of this period mention Assyria.[69] Our sources of information which do mention Necho's name are Egyptian and classical neither of which deals with the episodes found in the Bible.

---

65 *Ant.* x. 6. 1 (84-86); cf. *Against Apion* i. 19 (135) where Berosus describes the enemy differently.

66 Wiseman, *op. cit.*, pp. 67-69; cf. D. N. Freedman, "The Babylonian Chronicle," *BA*, XIX (1956), 51-52.

67 *ANET*, pp. 294-297; cf. p. 303.

68 E. Schrader, *The Cuneiform Inscriptions and the Old Testament*, trans. by O. C. Whitehouse (London: Williams and Norgate, 1885), II, 43.

69 Gardiner, *op. cit.*, p. 341.

Necho's accession date is established by the Apis stele from Egypt.[70] A stele in the Louvre represents him in the presence of the Thebian triad, and a scarab in Cairo commemorates his military exploits.[71]

Though it does not contain his name, it has been conjectured that the Aramaic letter found in 1942 at Saqqara is addressed to Necho II.[72] A figure named Adon appeals to pharaoh for aid against the king of Babylon who has advanced to Aphek. We do not know the outcome of the appeal.

In addition to his unfortunate military enterprises mentioned above, Necho also undertook engineering projects. According to Herodotus, he began the excavation of a canal to connect the Nile with the Red Sea, but after the loss of 120,000 lives, he abandoned the effort when he had been cautioned by an oracle that the work would benefit only the barbarians.[73] The canal project was later renewed by Darius and eventually completed by Ptolemy (285-246 B.C.).[74] Using Phoenician sailors, it is likely also that Necho's ships, sailing southward, rounded the Cape of Good Hope. Expressing personal doubts about the matter Herodotus reports, "In sailing around Libya they had the sun on their right hand."[75] After three years they returned home by way of the Strait of Gibralter.[76]

HOPHRA

Though Hophra's name occurs in only one Biblical passage, a great deal can be deduced from other passages that discuss Egyptian-Judean relations at this period. In all of these passages the ruler is merely called "pharaoh." Both Ezekiel and Jeremiah are as pessimistic about the help to be gained from Egypt in the Babylonian crisis as their predecessor Isaiah had been one hundred years before in the face of the Assyrian danger.

Pharaoh Hophra, early in his reign, invaded Palestine and

---

70 *Ibid.*, p. 357.
71 P. G. Elgood, *The Later Dynasties of Egypt* (Oxford: Basil Blackwell, 1951), p. 92.
72 H. L. Ginsberg, "An Aramaic Contemporary of the Lachish Letters," *BASOR*, No. 111 (1948), 24-27; John Bright, "A New Letter in Aramaic, Written to a Pharaoh of Egypt," *BA*, XII (1949), 46-52; A. Dupont-Sommer, "Un papyrus araméen d'époque saïte découvert a Saqqarah," *Semitica*, I (1948), 43-68.
73 Herodotus *Histories* ii. 158.
74 Diodorus Siculus *Library of History* i. 33. 9-12.
75 *Histories* iv. 42.
76 *Ibid.*

Phoenicia and incited Zedekiah to revolt against Babylon (Jer. 37:5). Even after the inevitable calamity was dawning, during the final siege of Jerusalem the pro-Egyptian party at the court of Judah continued to place its hope in Egyptian help. Indeed the advance of the Egyptian army brought about a temporary lifting of the siege and Nebuchadnezzar's army withdrew to deal with the Egyptian menace. Jeremiah remained adamant. The city was doomed. No hope could be expected from Egypt, for the Egyptian army would return to its own land (Jer. 37: 5 ff.). If there were only wounded Chaldeans left in their camp, they would rise up and burn the city of Jerusalem (Jer. 37:10).

In the face of optimism stirred up by false prophets in Babylon, Ezekiel is no less explicit. A prophecy dated on the twelfth day of the tenth month of the tenth year (January, 587 B.C.) compares Pharaoh to a monster in the Nile who claims the Nile for his own and claims that he made it, but who will be caught with hooks and cast into the wilderness to become food for scavenger beasts and birds (Ezek. 29:1 ff.). Three months later in an oracle dated on the seventh of the first month of the eleventh year (i.e., April, 586 B.C.), four months before the fall of Jerusalem, the prophet announces that God has broken the arm of Pharaoh so that it cannot be bound up to wield the sword. The Egyptians will be scattered among the nations. The arms of the king of Babylon will be strengthened and Pharaoh will groan before him like a man mortally wounded (Ezek. 30:20-26).

After the capitulation of Jerusalem the sons of Zedekiah were slaughtered in Zedekiah's presence; he himself was blinded and carried off to Babylon. For a brief period Gedaliah served as governor. Following the murder of Gedaliah, Hophra received a few Jewish refugees, including Jeremiah, into the delta city of Tahpanhes (probably Daphnae) (Jer. 43:7). Even in Egypt, Jeremiah continued his denunciation of Hophra. Among his last oracles we find:

> Thus says the Lord: Behold I will give Pharaoh Hophra king of Egypt into the hands of his enemies and into the hand of those who seek his life, as I gave Zedekiah king of Judah into the hand of Nebuchadrezzar king of Babylon, who was his enemy and sought his life (Jer. 44:30).

Pharaoh Hophra (588-569 B.C.), called *Wahibpre* by the Egyptians, *Uaphris* by Manetho,[77] and *Apries* by the Greeks, was of

---

77 *Op. cit.*, pp. 170-171.

the Twenty-sixth Egyptian Dynasty and succeeded his father Psammetichus II on the throne. His nineteen year reign[78] began only one year before the capitulation of Jerusalem to Nebuchadnezzar. Hophra seems to have envisioned himself in the role of re-establishing Egyptian sovereignty over the Middle East as numerous predecessors had attempted. His aid to Zedekiah is not mentioned in Egyptian sources.

Herodotus, who visited Egypt about one hundred years after the rule of Apries, reported the army campaign of Apries against Sidon and a sea battle against Tyre.[79] Apries, Herodotus reports, supposed that even a god could not depose him, but the situation changed when a defeat in Cyrene (ca. 570 B.C.) brought him into disfavor, particularly with the friends of the slain. Apries was deposed about 569 B.C. and was succeeded by Amasis who, according to Diodorus, had been sent by Apries to effect reconciliation. Amasis, however, turned coat, joined in the revolt and was then chosen king. In a pitched battle with Amasis, Apries was defeated.[80] After a time Amasis turned Apries over to his enemies; he was strangled by them and was then buried in the burial place of his fathers.[81] His successor reports that his burial was "that the enmity of the gods might be removed from him."[82] The stele in which Amasis records his victory over Apries is preserved in Cairo.[83]

Josephus, in surveying the period, while adding a few details to the Biblical account, merely reports that Zedekiah broke his treaty with the Babylonians and went over to the Egyptians, which act brought on the siege of Jerusalem. He continues:

> When the Egyptian king heard of the plight of his ally Sacchias, he raised a large force and came to Judaea to end the siege. Thereupon the Babylonian king left Jerusalem and went to meet the Egyptians and encountering them in a battle defeated and put them to flight and drove them out of the whole of Syria.[84]

In 1909 the British School of Archaeology in Egypt reported finding the palace of King Apries on the site of Memphis, the

---

78 *Ibid.*; Diodorus gives twenty-two years, *Library of History* i. 68. 1-5.
79 *Histories* ii. 161; Diodorus Siculus *Library of History* i. 68. 1.
80 Diodorus Siculus *Library of History* i. 68. 1-5.
81 Herodotus *Histories* ii. 169.
82 H. R. Hall, "The Restoration of Egypt," *CAH*, III, 303; J. H. Breasted, *Ancient Records of Egypt* (New York: Russell & Russell, 1906, reprinted 1962), IV, No. 997 f.
83 Elgood, *op. cit.*, p. 102, n. 1.
84 *Ant.* x. 7. 3 (110).

capital of Egypt.[85] Apries' head in a Corinthian helmet is represented on a small Naucratite vase — an aryballos — on which his name is written in hieroglyphics.[86] There is also a stele dated *ca.* 580 B.C. which depicts him offering bowls of wine to a god.[87]

SUMMARY

With Hophra the period of contact of the Old Testament with Egypt concludes. We lose sight of those Jews who went to Egypt in the time of Jeremiah. The interest of the writers of the Bible is in the fate and future of those Jews who went to Babylon. They composed the post-exilic community. Had Old Testament history continued through the late Persian and Greek periods, doubtless there might have been other figures, but as it is, with Hophra the story comes to an end.

From this area we have accumulated a list of four rulers: Shishak, Tirhakah, Necho, and Hophra of whom we can speak with confidence. So, king of Egypt, remains a debated figure.

---

85 T. Nicol, "Pharaoh Hophra," *ISBE*, IV, 2359.
86 Hall, *op. cit.*, p. 302, n. 2.
87 J. D. Douglas, *The New Bible Dictionary* (Grand Rapids: Eerdmans, 1962), p. 536, Fig. 107.

II

THE ROD OF GOD'S ANGER

Palestine, located between the major powers of the Middle East, was destined to be dominated in most of its history either by Mesopotamia or by Egypt. Assyria was extending her dominion at the expense of decadent Egypt just in the time corresponding to the period of the Israelite and Judean kingdoms. Nineteenth century explorers and excavators — Layard, Botta, and Rassam and their more recent successors — had good fortune in discovering the palaces of the Assyrian kings and their extensive records. These records were subsequently deciphered and published. All these factors make it inevitable that the major concentration of Biblical characters about whom there is material from external sources should be Assyrian and those with whom the Assyrians dealt. Though the Bible's primary interest is the story of the chosen nation and its role in salvation history, the clash of Assyrian might with the kings of Israel and Judah and its dominance over them makes it unavoidable that Assyria's kings should enter into the Biblical story.

The territorial expansions of Saul, David, and Solomon, were made possible because of a period of decadence in Mesopotamia which at that point suffered serious invasions from the Arameans. Despite the fact that Tiglath-pileser I (ca. 1000 B.C.) advanced to the sea, no effort was made at that time to hold the West. It was not until the reign of Ashurnasirpal II (883-855 B.C.) that Assyria became a real force in the West, and not until the time of Ahab, at the battle of Qarqar in 853 B.C., did she directly clash with Israel. At that time Ahab and his allies faced Shalmaneser III. Later Jehu paid him tribute. The Bible is chiefly concerned at this point with the jeopardy into which faith in Jehovah was brought by the innovations of

33

Jezebel. It takes notice neither of Ahab's war nor of Jehu's vassalage.

It has been conjectured that in the conflict of Jehoahaz with Ben-hadad III (or II?) the phrase, "Therefore the Lord gave Israel a savior, so that they escaped from the hand of the Syrians" (II Kings 13:5), is an allusion to Adad-nirari III (810-807 B.C.) who lists "Tyre, Sidon, Israel (*mat Hu-um-ri*), Edom, Palestine (*Pa-la-as-tu*), as far as the Setting Sun"[1] among those who paid him tribute. If the conjecture is valid, it is the first reference in the Bible to an Assyrian king.[2] The Tell al Rimah stele which mentions tribute he took from "*Ia'asu* (Joash) the Samaritan" is further evidence for his activities in the western region.[3]

With the rise of Tiglath-pileser III the power of Assyria was renewed, and Assyria really became dominant in Palestinian affairs. Every Assyrian king who reigned in the one hundred twenty-one year period from 747 to 626 B.C. is mentioned in the Bible.

TIGLATH-PILESER III

Though the clash between Israel and expanding Assyria was inevitable, the immediate cause of the intervention of Assyrians was the invitation of the Israelite kings themselves who sought aid in their problems and who traded, in the words of Isaiah, "the waters of Shiloah that flow gently" for the "waters of the Euphrates" (Isa. 8:5-7).

Menahem of Israel, following his assassination of Shallum, sought the aid of Tiglath-pileser to help him confirm his grasp on royal power. He proceeded to levy a tax of fifty shekels on every wealthy man of Israel in order to raise the needed money. Having received such a payment, the Assyrians withdrew from the land (II Kings 15:19-20).

A more lasting intervention was brought about at the invitation of Ahaz, king of Judah. In what is called the "Syro-Ephraimitic War," Pekah and Rezin plotted to replace Ahaz on the throne with the "son of Tabeel" and came up to besiege Jerusalem unsuccessfully (Isa. 7:6; II Kings 16:5). Against the stern advice of Isaiah (Isa. 7-8), Ahaz, at the price of a large gift

---

1 *ANET*, p. 281.

2 W. W. Hallo, "From Qarqar to Carchemish: Assyria and Israel in the Light of New Discoveries," *BA*, XXIII (1960), 42, n. 44.

3 Stephanie Page, "A Stela of Adad-Nirari III and Nergal-Eres from Tell al Rimah," *Iraq*, XXX (1968), 148-150.

of silver and gold, obtained jointly from the temple and from the king's house, invited Tiglath-pileser to relieve him:

> I am your servant and your son. Come up, and rescue me from the hand of the king of Syria and from the hand of the king of Israel who are attacking me (II Kings 16:7).[4]

As a result, Damascus fell, its people were exiled, Rezin was killed, and Ahaz went to Damascus to meet Tiglath-pileser and to become his vassal (II Kings 16:10). No doubt benefits were received, but Isaiah warned that Ahaz was creating more serious problems (Isa. 7-8), and the writer of Chronicles remarks that Tiglath-pileser afflicted Ahaz instead of strengthening him (II Chron. 28:20).

It was at this time also that Tiglath-pileser (also called Pul: II Kings 15:19; I Chron. 5:26) exiled sections of the northern kingdom:

> In the days of Pekah king of Israel, Tiglath-pileser king of Assyria came and captured Ijon, Abel-beth-maacah, Janoah, Kedesh, Hazor, Gilead, and Galilee, all the land of Naphtali; and he carried the people captive to Assyria (II Kings 15:29).

---

4 Cf. II Chron. 28:16; Josephus *Ant.* ix. 12. 3 (252).

3. TIGLATH-PILEZER III in a war chariot, on a relief at Ashtaroth. Courtesy, British Museum

The later account in Chronicles reads:

> So the God of Israel stirred up the spirit of Pul king of Assyria, and the spirit of Tiglath-pileser king of Assyria, and he carried them away, namely, the Reubenites, the Gadites, and the half-tribe of Manasseh, and brought them to Halah, Habor, Hara, and the river Gozan to this day (I Chron. 5:26; cf. 5:6).

A comprehensive survey of all the evidence for the life and activities of Tiglath-pileser III (745-727 B.C.), usurper of the throne,[5] lies outside the scope of this study. That Tiglath-pileser and Pulu (as his name is spelled in Babylonian records) are the same figure is established by the fact that he is called by one name in the Babylonian King List and by the other in the Babylonian Chronicle.[6] Layard discovered his palace — the center palace — in the mound of Nimrud between 1845 and 1847, but other of his reliefs were found in the southwest palace.[7] The British archaeologist Mallowan began re-excavation of this mound in 1949.[8]

With Tiglath-pileser III the Assyrian program of expansion recovered from the lapse it had suffered under his predecessors, and the basis for the Assyrian empire was laid. He campaigned in the West to put down an uprising instigated by Azariah of Judah,[9] and both Menahem[10] and Ahaz[11] are listed among those who paid him tribute. Pekah and Rezin felt his power. Pekah surrendered, but Damascus was captured by him in 732 B.C., and its people were exiled.[12] In Israel, following the death of Pekah, Hoshea gained his throne with Tiglath-pileser's permission.[13] All of these persons are mentioned in the records of Tiglath-pileser and all of these events will be dealt with in greater detail later in this study under the names of the individuals concerned.

---

5 Hallo, op. cit., p. 47; A. S. Anspacher, Tiglath Pileser III (New York: Columbia University Press, 1912; reprinted New York: AMS Press Inc., 1966), 72 pp.

6 E. R. Thiele, The Mysterious Numbers of the Hebrew Kings (Chicago: University of Chicago Press, 1951), p. 77.

7 A. H. Layard, Nineveh and Its Remains (London: John Murray, 1849), I, 19 ff.

8 M. E. Mallowan, Nimrud and Its Remains (London: Collins, 1966), 3 vols.

9 ANET, p. 282; see infra: "Uzziah."

10 ANET, pp. 283-284.

11 Ibid., p. 282.

12 Ibid., p. 283.

13 Ibid., p. 284.

4. RELIEF DEPICTING TIGLATH-PILESER III, Biblical Pul who took a
part of the Northern Kingdom into exile. Courtesy, British Museum

Tiglath-pileser put into effect the policy that became standard for his successors — that of exiling large segments of conquered populations.[14] Of one campaign he reports:

> [I deported] 30,300 inhabitants from their cities and settled
> them in the province of the town Ku [. . .]; 1,223 inhabi-
> tants I settled in the province of the Ullaba country.[15]

As previously noted, both Damascus and portions of Israel experienced this fate at his hands. The annals found at Calah re-

14 *Ibid.*, p. 283.
15 *Ibid.*

port: "Israel (lit.: "Omri-Land"; *Bit Humria*) . . . all its inhabitants (and) their possessions I led to Assyria."[16] In Josephus' account of the fall of Damascus he adds to the Scriptural account the detail, "He . . . brought over some of the Assyrian tribes and settled them in Damascus."[17]

→ Following a rebellion in Babylonia in 731 B.C., Tiglath-pileser "took the hand of Bel" in 729 and had himself set up as Pulu, king of Babylon.[18] It is by this name that he appears in the King Lists.[19]

A Nimrud bas-relief, now in the British Museum, represents Tiglath-pileser in the stylized Assyrian pattern.[20]

SHALMANESER V

Following the death of Tiglath-pileser III, Hoshea, king of Israel, became vassal of Shalmaneser V, son and successor to Tiglath-pileser, and paid him tribute. But when Hoshea, doubtless plotting for independence, ceased to pay his tribute and sent messengers to So, king of Egypt, Shalmaneser shut up Hoshea in prison and besieged Samaria for three years, after which (in the ninth year of Hoshea) it fell and its people were exiled to "Halah, and on the Habor, the river of Gozan, and in the cities of the Medes" (II Kings 17:1-6). A second text is more explicit:

> In the fourth year of King Hezekiah, which was the seventh year of Hoshea, son of Elah, king of Israel, Shalmaneser king of Assyria came up against Samaria and besieged it and at the end of three years he took it (II Kings 18:9-10).

Though he inserts a few variants, Josephus practically repeats the Biblical account.[21]

Shalmaneser V (726-722 B.C.) left behind no known inscriptions.[22] Outside the Biblical information just cited, his activities are known from the Babylonian Chronicle. His name also occurs in the Ptolemaic canon (#5) and occurs in the Babylonian King List as *Ululaia*.[23] A boundary stone (*kudurru*) dates an

---

16 *Ibid.*, p. 284.
17 *Ant.* ix. 12. 3 (253).
18 Hallo, *op. cit.*, pp. 50-51.
19 *ANET*, p. 272.
20 *ANEP*, No. 445.
21 Josephus *Ant.* ix. 14. 1 (277-279).
22 That inscription conjectured by Luckenbill (*ARAB*, I, 829) to be Shalmaneser's is now attributed to Esarhaddon; see Hallo, *op. cit.*, p. 51, n. 93.
23 *ANET*, p. 272.

event as happening in his third year;[24] also, a bronze weight has the inscription: "Palace of Shalmaneser (V), king of Ashur, two-thirds mina of the king."[25]

Josephus, claiming as his source the Tyrian archives, tells of Shalmaneser's overrunning Phoenicia. Sidon, Acre, and Tyre on the mainland abandoned allegiance to Tyre and recognized the authority of Assyria. Shalmaneser attacked island Tyre with sixty ships and eight hundred oarsmen. Although his fleet was dispersed, he nevertheless succeeded in maintaining a blockade for five years.[26]

A standing question in Old Testament study has been that of the role of Shalmaneser in the fall of Samaria. The Eponym List gives the main campaign of 725-723 B.C. as that directed against Samaria,[27] but his successor, Sargon, in a number of texts claims credit for exiling Samaria, and many scholars have been inclined to accept Sargon's claims.[28] The role of Sargon is not mentioned in the account of the book of Kings. Though the term used is in several instances merely "the king of Assyria," the context would seem plainly to imply Shalmaneser, and II Kings 18:9-10 is explicit in naming him. The Babylonian Chronicle, written some centuries after Shalmaneser, reports:

> On the twenty-fifth of Tebet Shalmaneser ascended the throne of Assyria. He destroyed Samaria.[29]

It is now assumed on the basis of this Chronicle that Samaria fell to Shalmaneser, perhaps in August or September, 722 B.C., and that Shalmaneser then died in December. Sargon completed the work of the exile, but also claimed credit for his predecessor's triumph.[30]

---

24 J. A. Brinkman, "A Preliminary Catalogue of Written Sources for a Political History of Babylonia: 1160-722 B.C.," *JCS*, XVI (1967), 102.
25 *ANEP*, No. 119.
26 *Ant.* ix. 14. 2 (283-287).
27 R. D. Barnett, *Illustrations of Old Testament History* (London: The British Museum, 1966), p. 52.
28 J. Bright, *A History of Israel* (Philadelphia: Westminster Press, 1959), p. 258; M. Noth, *The History of Israel* (London: A. and C. Black, 1958), p. 262; N. H. Snaith, "The First and Second Books of Kings," *IB*, III, 278-279; Sidney Smith, "The Supremacy of Assyria," *CAH*, III, 42; S. H. Cook, "Israel and the Neighboring States," *CAH*, III, 383.
29 *Babylonian Chronicle* i, 27-28; translation of H. Tadmor, "The Campaigns of Sargon II of Assur: A Chronological-Historical Study," *JCS*, XII (1958), 39.
30 Hallo, *op. cit.*, p. 51.

SARGON II

The relation of Sargon with Israel and Judah is passed over in complete silence by the writers of the books of Kings and Chronicles. Were it not for a sole, brief allusion in dating an act of Isaiah, Sargon would have completely escaped notice:

> In the year that the commander in chief, who was sent by Sargon the king of Assyria, came to Ashdod and fought against it and took it (Isa. 20:1).

In the face of this danger, Isaiah went naked and barefoot three years as a sign and portent against Egypt and Ethiopia, signifying that the king of Assyria would take away Egyptian and Ethiopian exiles.

The revolution in knowledge about Sargon (722-705 B.C.) began with the discovery of Sargon's palace at Khorsabad by Paul Emile Botta in 1843. Sargon had erected a new palace and had decorated its walls with reliefs illustrating his campaigns.[31] A text has been published which declares that Sargon was a son of Tiglath-pileser rather than the usurper he was formerly thought to have been.[32]

It is beyond the scope of this study to trace out the many campaigns of Sargon.[33] Two episodes in his life are of chief interest to us. First is the exiling of Samaria, and second is his Ashdod campaign. We have earlier implied that Sargon explicitly claims credit for the capture of Samaria despite the evidence now available in agreement with the Old Testament that attributes this victory to Shalmaneser. Sargon's claim is made in a number of texts:

(a) A pavement at the gate proclaims:

> (Sargon) conquerer of Samaria (*Samirina*) and of the entire country of Israel (*Bit Huumria*).[34]

(b) Annals of room XIV declare:

> I conquered and sacked the towns of Shinuhtu (and) Samaria, and all Israel.[35]

---

31 *Ibid.*, pp. 54-55.
32 A. Parrot, *Nineveh and the Old Testament* (London: S.C.M. Press, 1955), p. 45, n. 2; Hallo, *op. cit.*, p. 52.
33 Cf. Tadmor, *op. cit.*, pp. 22-40, 77-100.
34 *ANET*, p. 284.
35 *Ibid.*, p. 285.

5. PROCESSION OF HORSES AND CAPTIVES from the southwestern wall of the corridor of Sargon's palace at Khorsabad. Courtesy, Oriental Institute

6. TWO EUNUCHS depicted on the walls of Sargon's palace at Khorsabad. Courtesy, Oriental Institute

In three texts, Sargon lists the number of captives he carried off:

(a) Display Inscription:

> I besieged and conquered Samaria (*Sa-me-ri-na*), led away as booty 27,290 inhabitants of it. I formed from among them a contingent of 50 chariots and made remaining (inhabitants) assume their (social) positions.[36]

(b) The Annals contains a fragmentary text of the same episode.[37]

(c) Sargon's Prism found by M. E. Mallowan at Nimrud in 1952-1953:

> [The man of Sa]maria, who with a king [hostile to] me had consorted together not to do service and not to bring tribute and they did battle: in the strength the great gods, my lords, I clashed with them. [2]7,280 persons with [their] chariots and the gods their trust, as spoil I counted. 200 chariots (as) my [royal] muster I mustered from among them. The rest of them I caused to take their dwelling in the midst of Assyria.[38]

Sargon claims to have resettled people in Samaria:

> [The town (Samaria) I] re[built] better than (it was) before and [settled] therein people from countries which [I] myself [had con]quered.[39]

This text is confirmed by the Prism of Sargon from Nimrud which reports:

> The city of Samaria I restored, and greater than before I caused it to become. People of lands conquered by my two hands I brought within it; my officer as prefect over them I placed, and together with the people of Assyria I counted them.[40]

Prior to the struggle with Ashdod to which Sargon sent his commander in chief (Isa. 20), Sargon had in a western campaign swept down the coast as far as Gaza. In this campaign

---

36 *Ibid.*, pp. 284-285.
37 *Ibid.*, p. 284.
38 C. J. Gadd, "Inscribed Prisms of Sargon II from Nimrud," *Iraq*, XVI (1954), 173-201; also cited in A. Parrot, *Samaria* (London: S.C.M. Press, 1958), p. 51.
39 *ANET*, p. 284.
40 Gadd, *op. cit.*, p. 180.

(720 B.C.) Samaria was recaptured and Judah paid tribute.[41] In 716 B.C. on another campaign, he settled captive Arabian tribes in Samaria.[42] A third campaign came when the revolt in the West was first organized by Aziru, who withheld his tribute and sent seditious messages to other kings in the area. The Assyrians replaced Aziru with his brother Ahimiti who shortly afterward was overthrown by Iamani.[43] When in 712 the Assyrians put down the revolt, it is possible that the Judean city, Azekah, surrendered before Ashdod did.[44] The campaign is covered both by Sargon's Annals[45] and by the "Display Inscription" from Khorsabad.[46] Though the Annals declare that Sargon personally led the campaign, the Eponym Chronicle for the year says that he "stayed in the land."[47] If this statement is reliable, it would be in agreement with Isaiah's statement that the commander-in-chief led the operation against Ashdod. Further material on Sargon's relations with Israel is a Calah letter, possibly from this date, which lists Judah along with Egypt, Gaza, Moab, Ammon, Edom, and Ekron as paying tribute.[48] On the occasion of the above mentioned campaign, a basalt victory stele was erected at Ashdod, fragments of which have been recovered in the excavations there.[49]

In addition to the cuneiform texts, Sargon is also known from palace art. A relief from Khorsabad (BM 118822) shows the king in life-size receiving his minister or other official.[50]

To the period between Sargon and Esarhaddon is to be dated a text listing tribute from Ammon, Moab, Judah, and Edom. That of Judah is "ten minas of silver."[51]

---

41 Hallo, op. cit., p. 53.
42 Ibid., p. 55.
43 ANET, p. 286.
44 N. Gottwald, All the Kingdoms of the Earth (New York: Harper and Row, 1964), p. 166; cf. H. Tadmor, "Philistia Under Assyrian Rule," BA, XXIX (1966), 94.
45 ANET, p. 286.
46 Tadmor, op. cit., p. 94.
47 Hallo, op. cit., p. 56.
48 Ibid., p. 56; but cf. Tadmor, op. cit., pp. 92-93, where it is listed merely as after 716 B.C.
49 M. Dothan, "Ashdod," IEJ, XIV (1964), 87; D. N. Freedman, "The Second Season at Ancient Ashdod," BA, XXVI (1963), 138; Tadmor, op. cit., p. 95; text published by H. Tadmor, "Fragments of a Stele of Sargon II from the Excavations of Ashdod," Eretz-Israel, VIII (1967), 75, 241-245.
50 Barrett, op. cit., pp. 52-53.
51 ANET, p. 301; cf. R. H. Pfeiffer, "Three Assyriological Footnotes to the Old Testament," JBL, XLVII (1928), 185 f.

SENNACHERIB

The three Biblical sources of information on Sennacherib are: (a) II Kings 18 and 19, largely parallel to Isaiah 36 and 37 (II Kings 18:14-16 is lacking in Isaiah), (b) II Chronicles 32, which recounts some events, and (c) certain oracles of Isaiah, which though not specifically mentioning Sennacherib, may be concerned with his invasion (e.g., chaps. 10, 22, etc.). Sennacherib invaded Judah in 701 B.C., the fourteenth year of Hezekiah, took the fortified cities, and besieged the city of Lachish. Envisioning a siege of Jerusalem, Hezekiah made con-

7. THREE CAPTIVES, possible Jews from Lachish, under guard of an Assyrian soldier. The captives are playing lyres. Relief from the wall of Sennacherib's palace. Courtesy, British Museum

siderable preparation, including changing the water system, repairing the wall, making weapons and shields, and appointing commanders over the people (II Chron. 32:3-6; cf. Isa. 22). From Lachish Sennacherib sent his officers — the Tartan, the Rabsaris, and the Rabshakeh — with an army to Jerusalem. Sennacherib's representatives were met by three of Hezekiah's officials. The Rabshakeh attempted to demoralize the Judeans by insisting that Hezekiah's revolt was hopeless. Mere words could not be resources and strategy of war. Should their hope be in help from Egypt, Egypt was a broken reed of a staff which would pierce the hand of the man who leans on it. Since they hoped to get chariots and horsemen from Egypt, the Rabshakeh offered to furnish them two thousand horses if they would put riders on them and they could then see if they could repulse the least among the Assyrian captains. Should they rely on God, the Rabshakeh insisted that God had been offended in the removing of the high places in Hezekiah's reform. He also claimed that he had been sent by God to destroy the land. He further insisted that since none of the gods of the nations had been effective in saving their people, neither could the Lord save Jerusalem. The Rabshakeh attempted to convince the Judeans that exile was not such a bad fate. They would have their lives, and the land to which they would go would be like their own land.

Isaiah assured Hezekiah that the King of Assyria would return to his own land where he would fall by the sword (II Kings 19:7). Hezekiah had stripped the temple and the king's house in order to acquire the three hundred talents of silver and thirty talents of gold demanded (II Kings 18:14-16; not mentioned in Isaiah). If a chronological order may be assumed in the narrative in Kings, the tribute was paid before the Rabshakeh appeared at Jerusalem.

At his return, the Rabshakeh found Sennacherib departed from Lachish and fighting at Libnah (II Kings 19:8). Meanwhile it would appear that Tirhakah, king of Ethiopia, made an effort to intervene, and some suspected disloyalty brought further demands on Hezekiah, this time by letter (II Kings 19:9). The burden of the letter was to repeat his declaration that other gods had not delivered their people. Jerusalemites should not let their God deceive them into thinking that He would deliver them.

Isaiah promised Hezekiah deliverance. Sennacherib would not besiege the city (II Kings 19:32-34). An angel of the Lord slew 185,000 Assyrians in the night, and Sennacherib departed and returned home. When worshipping in the house of Nisroch his god, Adrammelech and Sharezer, his sons, slew him and escaped into the land of Ararat (II Kings 19:37; Isa. 37:37-38; II Chron. 32:21).

→ Sennacherib came to the throne of Assyria in 705 B.C. His palace was discovered by A. H. Layard at Quyunjiq (Nineveh) in 1847. There are now extant five whole or fragmentary copies of Sennacherib's annals in which he recounts his campaign against Hezekiah. A translation of the "Taylor Prism" is to be found in Thomas;[52] a translation of the "Oriental Institute Prism" is in Pritchard;[53] and the new "Nimrud Prism" is in Grollenberg.[54] These supplement the Biblical story in that they give the causes — which the Bible does not — for Sennacherib's punitive expedition. Hezekiah had allowed himself to be drawn into a general uprising of Philistia and had imprisoned Padi, king of Ekron. In general these accounts mentioned above parallel the first part of the Biblical account of Hezekiah's crisis, but not the second part.

In addition, a bull inscription from Nineveh records: "I laid waste the large district of Judah and made the overbearing and proud Hezekiah, its king, bow in submission."[55] A text from Nebi Yunus proclaims: "I laid waste the large district of Judah and put the straps of my (yoke) upon Hezekiah, its king."[56]

Sennacherib's siege of Lachish is depicted in the relief from Nineveh, now in the British Museum, which proclaims: "Sennacherib, king of the world, king of Assyria, sat upon a *nimedu* — throne and passed in review the booty (taken) from Lachish (*La-ki-su*)."[57] On the relief various stages of the siege are depicted. The archers attack the city, which defends itself. Some captives have been impaled; some beg for mercy; others depart the gate of the city with their bundles of the exile on their shoulders.

Assyrian sources do not recount the destruction of Sennacherib's army. One would hardly expect the boasting Assyrian monuments to do so. However, Herodotus relates:

> So presently came king Sanacharib against Egypt, with a great host of Arabians and Assyrians, and the warrior Egyptians

---

52 D. W. Thomas, *Documents from Old Testament Times* (London: Nelson, 1958), pp. 66-67.

53 *ANET*, p. 288.

54 L. H. Grollenberg, *Atlas of the Bible,* trans. by J. M. H. Reed (London: Nelson, 1956), pp. 88-89.

55 *ANET*, p. 288; Thomas, *op. cit.*, p. 68.

56 Thomas, *op. cit.*, p. 68.

57 See *ANET*, p. 288; Thomas, *op. cit.*, pp. 69-70.

would not march against him. The priest, in this quandary, went into the temple shrine and there bewailed to the god's image the peril which threatened him. In his lamentation he fell asleep, and dreamt that he saw the god standing over them and bidding him take courage, for he should suffer no ill by encountering the host of Arabia: "Myself," said the god, "will send you champions." So he trusted the vision, and encamped at Pelusium with such Egyptians as would follow him, for here is the road into Egypt; and none of the warriors would go with him, but only hucksters and artificers and traders. Their enemies too came thither, and one night a multitude of field mice swarmed over the Assyrian camp and devoured their quivers and their bows and the handles of their shields likewise, insomuch that they fled the next day unarmed and many fell. And at this day a stone statue of the Egyptian king stands in Hephaestus' temple, with a mouse in his hand, and an inscription to this effect: "Look on me, and fear the gods."[58]

The way in which all this material — in particular that not parelleled in Assyrian sources — fits together is a major question in Old Testament study. The crux of the problem centers around the figure of Tirhakah, king of Ethiopia. As earlier noted in dealing with Tirhakah, the accepted chronology would place his birth at 709 B.C. and the beginning of his co-regency in 690/689 B.C. Such a birthdate would make it impossible for him to have led an army in 701 B.C.

As we have seen in the previous chapter, three major alternatives have been proposed in the effort to deal with this problem. The first assumes that there is an anachronism or other error in Isaiah's reference to Tirhakah.[59] The second assumes an earlier date for Tirhakah's birth and insists that he is proleptically called king in the account when he was at the time of the event only a general. Later he became king. On this basis, then, one campaign of Sennacherib which ended in failure is espoused.[60] A third alternative assumes that there were two campaigns of Sennacherib and that the Old Testament has telescoped the two into one. The first was in 701 B.C., and the second was considerably later (about fifteen years) when Tirhakah was king of Ethiopia. It was at this later time that Sennacherib's army was destroyed. This last case was expounded by W. F. Albright[61]

---

58 *Histories* ii. 141.

59 Noth, *op. cit.*, p. 268; H. H. Rowley, "Hezekiah's Reform and Rebellion." *BJRL*, LXIV (1962), 395 ff.

60 Thomas, *op. cit.*, pp. 64-65.

61 "Further Light on Synchronisms between Egypt and Asia in the Period 935-685 B.C.," *BASOR*, No. 141 (1956), 25 f.

and more recently by Siegfried H. Horn,[62] and by Samuel J. Schultz.[63] It has the admitted difficulties that Assyrian sources know of no second campaign and also that such a campaign is difficult to fit into the career of Hezekiah.

Advocates of alternative number two must assume that there was a lapse of time of some twenty years — not indicated in Scripture — between the destruction of Sennacherib's army in 701 B.C. and his death in 681 B.C. About the death of Sennacherib, the Babylonian Chronicle states: "On the twentieth of the month of Tebet, his son killed Sennacherib, king of Assyria, during a rebellion."[64] Ashurbanipal, Sennacherib's grandson, tells of punishing his murderers:

> As a posthumous offering at this time I smashed the rest of the people alive by the very figures of the protective deities between which they had smashed Sennacherib, my grandfather.[65]

ADRAMMELECH

Adrammelech is listed in the parallel accounts in II Kings 19: 37 and Isaiah 37:38 as one who joined with Sharezer in slaying Sennacherib.

Eusebius quoted a statement to the effect that this king was murdered by his son Adramelus and was succeeded by Nergilus, who was executed by Axerdis.[66] By Josephus the name is given as Andromachos.[67]

The Babylonian Chronicle states that Sennacherib was slain by his son, but gives no name.[68] Likewise Ashurbanipal comments on the death of his father and his own punishment of the murderers in 648 B.C. when he took Babylon, but fails to give names.[69]

It has been suggested by P. Dhorme that Adrammelek is the son of Sennacherib, who is called Arad-Belit or Arad-Malkat in Assyrian sources.[70]

---

62 "Did Sennacherib Campaign Once or Twice Against Hezekiah?" *Andrews University Seminary Studies,* IV (1966), 1-28.

63 *The Old Testament Speaks* (New York: Harper and Bros., 1960), pp. 213-214. See also the summary in P. Van Der Meer, *The Chronology of Western Asia* (Leiden: E. J. Brill, 1955), pp. 81-82.

64 Thomas, *op. cit.,* p. 72.

65 *Ibid.,* p. 72; see Hallo, *op. cit.,* p. 59, n. 145, for bibliography.

66 *Chronicle* i. 9 (*P.G.* 19, 123; *G.C.S.* 20, 18).

67 *Ant.* x. 1. 5 (23).

68 Thomas, *op. cit.,* p. 72.

69 *ANET,* p. 288.

70 "Les pays bibliques et l'Assyrie," *RB,* VII (1910), 520.

SHAREZER

Sharezer (II Kings 19:37; Isa. 37:38), as we have just mentioned above, joined with Adrammelech in the assassination of Sennacherib. This figure is called Seleukaros by Josephus.[71]

Dhorme conjectured that this figure is Nabusharuzur, one of the officers whose name, in its full form, in the lists denoted the year 682-681 B.C.[72]

ESARHADDON

Esarhaddon succeeded to the throne following the assassination of his father Sennacherib (II Kings 19:37; Isa. 37:38) by the other sons. Following the return from exile, "the adversaries of Judah and Benjamin" approach Zerubbabel and Jeshua wishing to aid in reconstructing the temple. They insist that they worship God: "We have been sacrificing to him ever since the days of Esarhaddon king of Assyria who brought us here" (Ezra 4:2).

The Babylonian Chronicle relates the accession of Esarhaddon under circumstances quite similar to those related in Scripture:

> On the 20th of the month of Tebet, his son killed Sennacherib, king of Assyria, during a rebellion. For 23 years Sennacherib had exercised kingship over Assyria. The rebellion continued from the 20th of the month of Tebet to the 2nd of the month of Adar. On the 18th of the month of Adar, Esarhaddon, his son, sat on the throne in Assyria.[73]

During his reign (680-669 B.C.) Esarhaddon devoted much attention to rebuilding the city of Babylon over which he ruled. Bricks of his have been found claiming renewal of the pavement and the temple tower of Esagila, the temple of Marduk in Babylon.[74] The Babylonian lists count him as full king, and in Babylon itself business documents were dated by his regnal years.[75]

By campaigns Esarhaddon established his authority in Persia, Media, and Arabia. According to tablets found at Calah in 1955, he forced his Iranian citizens in 672 B.C. to support the succes-

---

71 *Ant.* x. 1. 5 (23).
72 *Op. cit.*, p. 520.
73 Thomas, *op. cit.*, p. 72.
74 A. T. Olmstead, *History of Assyria* (Chicago: University of Chicago, 1951), p. 350.
75 *Ibid.*, p. 357.

8. STELE DEPICTING ESARHADDON as the Great King with suppliants bowed before him. Courtesy, Aleppo Museum

sion of his sons in Assyria and Babylon after his death. Scholars have been quick to call attention to the parallels in form of these vassal treaties to Old Testament covenants.[76] Esarhaddon's palace was excavated at Calah by A. H. Layard. Layard termed it "the palace of Nimrud."[77]

The chief drive of Esarhaddon's reign seems to have been

76 D. J. Wiseman, "The Vassal-Treaties of Esarhaddon," *Iraq*, XX/1 (1958), 1-27; Hallo, *op. cit.*, p. 60.
77 *Op. cit.*, II, 26 ff.

toward Egypt. En route he passed by Haran where he received a favorable omen from the moon god, Sin. He began the siege of Tyre, which was allied with Egypt, in 673 B.C. Pressing on to Egypt, he clashed with forces of Tirhakah. Though he met with initial defeat, eventually he forced Tirhakah to retreat into upper Egypt. Memphis was captured, and the family and property of Tirhakah were taken.[78] Esarhaddon assumed the new title "King of kings, king of Egypt"[79] and was the first king of Assyria to use the title. When in 669 Tirhakah's further revolt forced him to undertake a second campaign in Egypt, Esarhaddon died on the way, and the army returned home.

At one point in his career Esarhaddon summoned twenty-two princes of Hatti land to Nineveh. It has been conjectured that it was on this occasion that Manasseh was taken to Babylon (II Chron. 33:11). At any rate, Esarhaddon does list "Manasseh king of Judah" with many other westerners who contributed material to the new palace at Nineveh.[80]

A text directly relevant to his importing of people into Samaria, mentioned above, has not been found. He, like his predecessors, does mention his policy of exiling peoples. Of Sidon he said:

> I led to Assyria his teeming subjects which could not be counted.[81]

And of Egypt he said:

> All Ethiopians I deported from Egypt — leaving not even one to do homage (to me).[82]

Esarhaddon, on returning from Egypt, set up a stele at Nahr-el-Kelb (Dog River in Lebanon), beside that of Ramses II,[83] and a second stele at Senjirli. On the latter, which was discovered in 1888 by the Germans and is in the Berlin Museum, the king is depicted with two of his enemies — Tirhakah of Egypt and perhaps Ba'lu of Tyre — on leashes attached to hooks in their lips.[84]

---

78 See earlier discussion of Tirhakah.
79 *ANET*, p. 290.
80 *Ibid.*, p. 291.
81 *Ibid.*
82 *Ibid.*, p. 293.
83 Cf. *ANET*, p. 293.
84 Text: *ANET*, p. 293; Illustration: *ANEP*, pp. 154, 300-301, No. 447.

Not possessed of an undue modesty, Esarhaddon said of himself and of his achievements: "I am powerful, I am all powerful, I am a hero, I am gigantic, I am colossal."[85]

ASHURBANIPAL

Ashurbanipal, son of Esarhaddon and the last significant king of Assyria, is mentioned only once in the Old Testament and that under the corrupted name Osnappar. Judeans of the post-exilic period are identified as having been imported into the land by him:

> Then wrote Rehum the commander, Shimshai the scribe, and the rest of their associates, the judges, the governors, the officials, the Persians, the men of Erech, the Babylonians, the men of Susa, that is, the Elamites, and the rest of the nations whom the great and noble Osnappar deported and settled in the cities of Samaria and in the rest of the province Beyond the River (Ezra 4:9-10; cf. I Esdras 2:16-25).

In the book of Kings, Ashurbanipal is not mentioned but importing of people into Samaria is attributed to an unnamed "king of Assyria" in II Kings 17:24.

Ashurbanipal's succession to the throne had been provided for by his father Esarhaddon before the latter's death (see above). This wise foresight did not, however, prevent later clashes with his brother Shamashshumukin who had been designated king of Babylon by Esarhaddon. Recent evidence found at Haran would imply that Ashurbanipal's rule lasted from 668 to 626 B.C.[86]

Ashurbanipal continued his father's conflicts with Tirhakah of Egypt (see Tirhakah) and was successful in that he penetrated into Egypt and destroyed Thebes in 663 B.C.[87] This event is recalled by the prophet Nahum (3:8). It was during this campaign that "twenty-two kings from the seashore, islands, and the mainland" were forced to accompany him with their "armed forces and their ships." Among these is "Manasseh, king of Judah."[88] Ashurbanipal also claims a second victorious campaign against Egypt[89] and one against Tyre.[90]

---

85 *ARAB*, II, No. 577.
86 C. J. Gadd, "The Harran Inscriptions of Nabonidus," *Anatolian Studies*, VIII (1958), 69-72.
87 *ANET*, p. 294.
88 *Ibid.*
89 *ARAB*, II, 295-296, Nos. 776-778.
90 *Ibid.*, II, 296, No. 779.

9. RELIEF FROM ASHURBANIPAL'S PALACE at Nineveh. The second register depicts a military band with drums, cymbals, and lyres. Courtesy, The Louvre

10. ASHURBANIPAL OF ASSYRIA depicted as he ceremonially begins the work of rebuilding a temple. Courtesy, British Museum

Some of Ashurbanipal's reliefs were discovered by Layard in the mound of Quyunjiq. Rassam and Loftus found others in Ashurbanipal's own palace — the northwest palace. Many of these were lost when a boat transporting them sank in the Tigris River. He is represented in art objects including that on the clay tablet which describes his building projects at Babylon.[91]

No doubt Ashurbanipal's most lasting contribution to civilization was the assembling of his great library in Nineveh which

91 *ANEP*, No. 450.

was brought to light in the excavations of Rassam in the last century. Here on clay tablets were preserved important documents of contemporary history as well as myths, legends, and epics of the past. These documents have opened to the world a knowledge of ancient Mesopotamia.

Ashurbanipal's records contain no specific statement about importing people into Palestine, but he did continue the policy established by his predecessors of exiling subject peoples. Of Elam he reports:

> Their gods, their people, their cattle, their sheep, their property, their goods, wagons, horses, mules, weapons, and implements of warfare, I carried off to Assyria.[92]

Again he says:

> For a (distance) of a month of twenty-five days' journey I devastated the provinces of Elam. Salt and *sihlu* (some prickly plant) I scattered over them. The daughters of the kings, the sisters of the kings, together with the older and younger (*lit.* earlier and later) (members) of the families of the Elamite kings, the prefects and mayors of all of those cities which I had conquered, the chiefs of the bowmen (archers), the "second" (-men of the chariots), the drivers (*lit.* holders of the reins), the "third"-riders (?) (of the chariots), the horsemen, the (light-armed?) bowmen, the captains and (heavy-armed?) bowmen of the whole army, all there were; the people, male and female, great and small; horses, mules, asses, cattle and sheep, which were more numerous than grasshoppers, I carried off to Assyria.[93]

It was he who captured Susa from whence some of the exiles mentioned in the Biblical passage came.[94]

With Ashurbanipal the story of Israel and the Assyrian kings comes to an end. His insignificant successors are not mentioned by name in the Old Testament. Following the death of Ashurbanipal, Josiah carried through his reform in 621 B.C. in which he cleansed Judah of evidence of foreign cult. Josiah's reform (II Kings 22-23) is usually interpreted (though the matter is not mentioned in the Old Testament) as also having political implications. In freeing his people from Assyrian religious influence, he was also freeing them from Assyrian political domination. An unnamed "king of Assyria" enters the Old Testament

---

92 *ARAB*, II, 307, No. 804; cf. 308, No. 808.
93 *Ibid.*, II, 310-311, No. 811.
94 Raymond Bowman, "Ezra," *IB*, III, 601.

story again when Necho went to his aid on the Euphrates in 609 B.C. From Babylonian sources we are able to deduce that the king was Ashur-uballit II. We have earlier seen how Josiah attempted to block Necho at Megiddo and was killed for his trouble (II Kings 23:29). Nineveh hastened to its downfall in 612 B.C. at the hands of the Babylonians, Medes, and Scythians, which event is the theme of oracles of Nahum (1-3) and Zephaniah (2:13-15). Specific figures do not appear in these oracles as the prophet taunts: "Your shepherds are asleep, O king of Assyria" (Nah. 3:18).

SUMMARY

By way of summary, the Old Testament notices the names of six Assyrian kings: Tiglath-pileser III, Shalmaneser V, Sargon II, Sennacherib, Esarhaddon, and Ashurbanipal. About all of these we have an abundance of information from Middle Eastern sources. In addition, two lesser figures — Adrammelech and Sharezer — are named, about whom we possibly have some information.

III

GOD RAISED UP FOR THEM ADVERSARIES

The uninitiated would assume that Israel's contacts with her fellow inhabitants of Syro-Palestine should have left some trace in the records of these regions. Palestinian discovery, however, has been exceptionally poor in inscriptional materials, and extant manuscript materials do not go back as far as the Old Testament period. The records of the Phoenicians, Philistines, Edomites, Moabites, and Arameans have, with few exceptions, not been forthcoming. No royal steles of the Israelite kings, and only one of any sort of Palestinian king during the Israelite period, have been found.[1] The period of contact with these peoples mentioned above also largely antedates the focal point of interest of the classical historians. There are, however, numerous names of kings and other rulers from Egyptian and Assyrian records, most of whom play no role in the Bible.

This section of our study deals with what is to be found concerning the immediate neighbors of Israel. No figure of the period of the conquest, of the judges, or of the united monarchy (with the exception of material transmitted by Josephus) is known outside the Bible and later sources that are dependent upon it. The current study then is limited to the period subsequent to the division of the monarchy.

THE PHILISTINES

Names of Philistines are not abundant in the Bible, and search for information on those names which do occur is particularly frustrating. A list of the known names was given by R. A. S. Macalister who characterized the list as "so meagre that

---

1 See Mesha, below.

it is scarcely worth discussing."[2] The patriarchs Abraham and Isaac had contact with Abimelech, king of Gerar, and Isaac dealt with his officials: Ahuzzath, his advisor, and Phicol, the commander of his army (Gen. 20:3; 26:1, 26). Samson had traffic with Delilah (Judg. 16:4 ff.);[3] David fought against Goliath of Gath (I Sam. 17:44 ff.; 22:10); and other related named giants (Ishbibenob, Saph, Goliath, and Lahmi) were slain by others (II Sam. 21:16-22; cf. I Chron. 20:5). When fleeing from Saul, David found safety in the area of Achish, king of Gath (I Sam. 21:10; 27:2 ff.). However, each of these characters just mentioned is known only from the Bible.

Assyrian records carry a sizeable list of kings of the Philistine cities in the later period following Assyria's entrance into the Palestinian picture. These kings were either vassals of Assyria or were in rebellion against her and are known from Assyria's records to have had contact with Israel, but not one of them is a Biblical figure.[4]

Excavations have been carried out in some of the Philistine cities — Tell-el-Hesi (Eglon), Tell Ashdod, and Tell Askelon — but the literature and records of the Philistines have not been found. Their language is as yet unknown.

THE EDOMITES

A list of the descendants of Esau is given in Genesis 36 together with a list of eight kings who reigned in Edom before there was a king in Israel (Gen. 36:31 ff.; cf. I Chron. 1:43-51). During the period of the wilderness wandering Edom's king is denominated merely "the King of Edom" (Num. 20:14-21). Doeg the Edomite was Saul's shepherd (I Sam. 21:7) and slew the priests of Nob (I Sam. 22:18). In the time of David, Hadad the Edomite, a later adversary to Solomon, fled to Egypt and was given in marriage the sister of Tahpenes the queen (I Kings 11:16 ff.). This woman bore him a son named Genubath before Hadad returned home at the news of the death of David. The Old Testament has ample evidence of a long-standing animosity between Israel and Edom which became all the keener as Edom joined Israel's adversaries at the time of the Exile (Ps. 137:7). The prophets Amos (1:11), Jeremiah (49:

---

2 *The Philistines Their History and Civilization* (London: Humphrey Milford, Oxford University Press, 1914), pp. 81-82.

3 *Ibid.*, p. 45, points out that Delilah may not have been a Philistine.

4 See H. Tadmor, "Philistia under Assyrian Rule," *BA*, XXIX (Sept., 1966), 86-102.

7-22). and Obadiah (1-21) give oracles against Edom. But the animosity against Edom is an animosity without personal names.

Few sites in the Edomite area have been excavated. Her language, literature, and records — if they existed — are as yet unknown to us. Some seventh century Edomite seals were found at Ezion Geber, one bearing the title "Qoscanal, servant of the King."[5] Isolated Edomite kings can be found in Assyrian accounts of Assyria's contacts with this region following Tiglathpileser III,[6] but they are not Biblical figures.

THE AMMONITES

The progenitors of the Ammonites are Lot and his son Benammi (Gen. 19:36-38). Moses faced Og, king of Bashan, who resided at Rabbah (Deut. 3:11; 31:4), and Sihon, king of Heshbon (Deut. 2:26, 30, etc.), who refused Israel passage through the land. Both were defeated by Israel. These kings in the land traditionally thought of as Ammonite are called Amorite kings (Num. 21:21; Deut. 31:4). The Amorites and Ammonites may have lived side by side with an overlap of territory. In the period of the judges, Jephthah won a victory over oppressing Ammonites whose individuals remain nameless (Judg. 10-11).

The siege of Ramoth-Gilead by Nahash the Ammonite stimulated Saul to assume the kingship to which he had been anointed by Samuel, and the deliverance of the besieged city was his first act of leadership (I Sam. 11:1 ff.). In David's time relations with the Ammonites seem to have been more friendly, and upon the occasion of Nahash's death David sent condolence to his newly crowned son, Hanun. Unfortunately, David's motive was misinterpreted; David's men were treated quite insultingly (II Sam. 10:1 ff.); the Ammonite war was touched off (II Sam. 10:3 ff.); and David subjugated the territory. Nahash seems to have had at least one other son whose name was Shobi and who later came to David when David fled from Absalom (II Sam. 17:27). One of Solomon's wives, Naamah, the mother of Rehoboam (I Kings 14:21, 31; II Chron. 12:13), was an Ammonitess. After the division of the kingdom, Judah's fortunes with Ammon vacillated, but personal names are lacking.

We next encounter an Ammonite name following the fall of Jerusalem when Baalis, the Ammonite king, plotted with Ishmael to slay Gedaliah, governor of Judah (Jer. 40:14). Finally,

---

5 Nelson Glueck, *The Other Side of the Jordan* (New Haven: American Schools of Oriental Research, 1940), p. 110.
6 *ANET*, p. 282.

following the exile, Nehemiah had problems with Tobiah the servant, the Ammonite (Neh. 2:10, 19; 4:3, 7, etc.).

Only a few sites in the Ammonite territory have been excavated, and the results of those have, with a few exceptions, not appeared in final form. We do know, however, Ammonite names from Assyrian records, from an inscription, and from a few seals. An Ammonite king Ba'sa, son of Ruhubi, participated along with Ahab and others in the battle of Qarqar in 853 B.C.[7] Later Sanipu, king of the Ammonites, paid tribute to Tiglath-pileser III in 733 B.C.[8] And Buduili paid tribute to Sennacherib.[9] Buduili's name also appears in the records of the next two Assyrian monarchs. His successor, Amminadbi, paid tribute to Ashurbanipal.[10]

The longest known Ammonite inscription is the fragmentary one on a statue found near the citadel of Ammon. Provisionally dated from the seventh century, it probably reads: "Yarahᶜazar, chief of the horse."[11] There are a few Ammonite seals with personal names. One reads "Adoni-pillet, servant of Ammi-nadab." Another belongs to "Adoni-nur, servant of Amminadab." It is likely that this is the Ammi-nadbi mentioned by Ashurbanipal. Other seals belong to Shavel; to Menahem, the son of Yenahem; to Alyah, maidservant of Hana'el; and to "ᶜNMWT, maidservant of DBLKS," and finally there is a stamp seal inscribed "Belonging to 'W', son of MR'L (Mar'il)."[12]

Other than the figure Tobiah, there is no point of contact between these various individuals and the named Biblical figures. Tobiah is treated in another context.

THE MOABITES

Early Moabites

Lot and his son Moab are the ancestors of the Moabites whose traditional territory is east of the Dead Sea between the Arnon River and the Brook Zered. Israel in her period of wandering faced Balak, the son of Zippor, who sought Balaam to curse Israel (Num. 22-24). The outcome of the conflict was a decree

---

7 *Ibid.*, p. 279.
8 *Ibid.*, p. 282.
9 *Ibid.*, p. 287.
10 *Ibid.*, p. 294.
11 G. Landes, "The Material Civilization of the Ammonites," *BA*, XXIV (1961), 79, 81.
12 N. Avigad, "An Ammonite Seal," *IEJ*, II (1952), 163 f.; Landes, *op. cit.*, pp. 81, 82, 84.

excluding the Moabites from the congregation forever (Deut. 23:3). Eglon, king of Moab, oppressed Israel in the period of the Judges and was slain by Ehud (Judg. 3:12-30). At this same general period the family of Elimelech sojourned in Moab, and the sons found wives in the Moabite women Ruth and Orpah (Ruth 1:4). Later David entrusted his parents to an unnamed king of Moab when fleeing from Saul (I Sam. 22:3-5). Still later Ithmah the Moabite was one of David's mighty men (I Chron. 11:46). David fought with and subdued the Moabites (II Sam. 8:2; I Chron. 18:2), and Solomon ruled over them. However, the only other Moabite mentioned by name in the Old Testament is Mesha, king of Moab (II Kings 3), whom we shall shortly notice in detail. During the period of the monarchy, Israelite kings had various clashes with Moab, and the prophets denounced Moab without mentioning personal names in their oracles. Near the end of the Israelite kingdom an unnamed king was reigning there (Jer. 27:3).

Moabite kings paid tribute to the Assyrians. Tiglath-pileser III received tribute from Salamanu of Moab;[13] Sennacherib from Kammusunadbi;[14] while Musuri, king of Moab, along with other kings (including the king of Judah), provided materials for Esarhaddon's palace at Nineveh.[15] Under the dominion of Ashurbanipal, a figure, Kamashaltu, ruled in Moab.[16]

For the most part the territory of Moab remains yet unexcavated. Some seasons have been carried out at Dhiban, the capital of the Moabite kingdom, at Khirbet Balucah, and at a few other sites in the Moabite area, but the final publications of the excavations have not yet appeared.

From this region it is only about Mesha that we have additional information for our purposes.

Mesha

Scripture does not preserve the circumstances by which the Moabites became subject to the kings of Israel, but they must have been conquered by Omri, as the Mesha stone claims, and must have been subjected to a heavy tribute in sheep and wool (II Kings 3:4). Following the death of Ahab, Mesha, king of Moab, revolted (II Kings 1:1), and the two Jewish kingdoms

---

13 *ANET,* p. 282.
14 *Ibid.,* p. 287.
15 *Ibid.,* p. 291.
16 *Ibid.,* p. 298.

11. THE MESHA STONE, more commonly known as the Moabite Stone. Courtesy, Oriental Institute

led by Jehoram (successor to Ahab) and Jehoshaphat formed an alliance to meet the challenge. After a general muster of the men of Moab, the two armies confronted each other, resulting in a preliminary victory for Israel and in the devastation of Edom: "And they overthrew the cities and on every good piece of land every man threw a stone, until it was covered; they stopped every spring of water and felled all the good trees; till only its stones were left in Kir-hareseth, and the slingers surrounded and conquered it" (II Kings 3:25). After being besieged, Mesha attempted to break through the lines of the enemy, but failed. In desperation at this defeat, he then "took his eldest son who was to reign in his stead, and offered him for a burnt offering upon the wall" (II Kings 3:27). Further details of the exchange are passed over in silence. Scripture ends its account of the affair with the simple statement: "And there came great wrath upon Israel; and they withdrew from him and returned to their own land" (II Kings 3:27). Moab was not resubjugated by Jehoram.

To contrast with the Israelite account of the exchange, we have the record preserved by Mesha himself upon a monument which we know as the Moabite (or Mesha) stone. This stone which was discovered by Klein, a Lutheran missionary, in 1868 in Dhiban, a city of the Moabites east of the Dead Sea, was acquired for the Louvre Museum by Clermont-Ganneau. It is the most significant monument of the Moabite kingdom, one of the longest Palestinian inscriptions yet recovered, and the only known victory stele of a Palestinian king of the Israelite period.

The inscription is dedicated to the god Chemosh giving him thanks for the Moabite victory over the Israelites. Mesha attributes the earlier humiliation of Moab to the anger of Chemosh and states that Omri occupied the land of Medeba (a city of Moab) and the territory north of the Arnon River. Like the scriptural account, Mesha mentions "flocks of the land" as a part of the tribute Moab had paid (1. 31), but the specific clashes he mentions are not alluded to in the Bible. According to Mesha, the land was occupied for forty years during the reign of Omri and half that of his son. At that time Mesha claims a great victory for himself: "I have triumphed over him and over his house, while Israel has perished forever."[17] Just as the Israelites gave credit to Yahweh for their victory, so Mesha gives credit to Chemosh for his. He claims under a commission from Chemosh to have captured Nebo, to have put its inhabitants under the ban, and to have carried off from there things belonging to Yahweh which things he proceeded to drag before Chemosh.

The inscription raises certain problems, one of which is chronological. The combined reigns of Omri and Ahab do not total the forty years Mesha mentions for the length of Moab's subjection. A second problem is that Scripture represents the revolt as taking place after the death of Ahab rather than before. One possibility of solution is that Mesha used the term "forty" as a round number. Another is that he, in describing his opponent, used "son" loosely for "descendant" as some Biblical passages do. If this be the case, Mesha's forty years can extend into the reign of Jehoram. The problem is treated in F. M. Cross, Jr. and David N. Freedman, *Early Hebrew Orthography* (New Haven: American Oriental Society, 1952), p. 39.

---

17 M. Noth, "Israelitische Stämme zwischen Ammon und Moab," *ZAW*, LX (1944), 42 ff.; A. H. Van Zyl, *The Moabites* (Leiden: Brill, 1960), pp. 139 ff.; 161 ff.; J. Liver, "The Wars of Mesha, King of Moab," *PEQ*, XCIX (1967), 14-31.

THE PHOENICIANS

Not until the time of David can it be demonstrated that Israel came into close relations with her neighbors to the north, the Phoenicians. Hiram, king of Tyre, furnished materials for the building of David's house (II Sam. 5:11; I Chron. 14:1) and still later entered a league with Solomon to supply materials for Solomon's building projects (I Kings 5:1 ff.). He also made major contributions to Solomon's shipping interests; his fleet brought gold from Ophir (I Kings 10:11; 9:27-28; II Chron. 9:10). In return Solomon paid Hiram annual fees and ceded to him twenty cities which did not prove satisfactory to Hiram (I Kings 9:11-14).

At this same period, yet another Hiram whose mother was a widow of Naphtali, but whose father was from Tyre, was brought from Tyre by Solomon to do the bronze work on the temple (I Kings 7:14 ff., 40 ff.; cf. II Chron. 2:12-13).

The latter of these two Tyreans is otherwise unknown, but as for the former, Josephus claims Menander as his source of information that Hiram came to the throne at the age of fifty-three and reigned thirty-four years (981-947 B.C.), then was succeeded by his thirty-six year old son Baal-Azari. During his years of reign he did building projects connected with the temples of Heracles and Astarte.[18] Josephus also cites a historian of Phoenicia, Dius (who is otherwise unknown), as a further source for information on Hiram's building activities and on an exchange of riddles with Solomon.[19] Considerably later another Hiram, king of Tyre, appears in the records of Tiglath-pileser III.[20]

At a period in Israelite history later than Solomon, Ahab took for a wife Jezebel, the daughter of Ithbaal, king of the Sidonians (I Kings 16:31). It has long been recognized that it is likely that this marriage was a political-commercial one. Josephus, again claiming the authority of Menander, informs us that a thirty-six year old priest of Ashtart, Ittobaal, brought to an end the line of Hiram in Tyre and became the dominant ruler in Phoenicia for thirty-two years (899-867 B.C.). He exchanged the title "King of Tyre" for that of "King of Sidon."[21]

---

18 *Against Apion* i. 18 (116 ff.); *Ant.* viii. 5. 3 (144-146); W. B. Fleming, *The History of Tyre* (New York: Columbia University Press, 1915; reprinted AMS Press, 1966), 166 pp.

19 *Against Apion* i. 112-115.

20 *ANET*, p. 283.

21 *Against Apion* i. 18 (116 ff.); *Ant.* viii. 13. 2 (324); cf. F. C. Eiselen, *Sidon, A Study in Oriental History* (New York: Columbia University Press, 1907; reprinted AMS Press, 1966), 172 pp.

The excavations in Tyre, up to this point, have not revealed material directly connected with either Hiram or with Ithbaal. At a much earlier period than David, names of Phoenicians are frequent in Egyptian sources; e.g., the Tell-el-Amarna letters and the Tale of Wen-Amon. The chief clashes of the Assyrians with the Phoenicians are later than David and Ahab. Names of kings such as that of Ba'lu of Tyre on the Senjirli stele of Esarhaddon do occur in these records, but the Bible has no Phoenician names from this period despite the fact that beginning with Amos a long line of prophets have oracles against Tyre.

THE ARAMEANS

Israel traced herself back to Aramean stock (Deut. 26:5) and in the patriarchal period Nahor, Bethuel, and Laban (Gen. 24:15) stand out as relatives of Israel in the area of Haran (Gen. 29:4 ff.). In the time of the Judges, Cushanrishathaim, "the king of Aram Naharaim," oppressed Israel until deliverance was wrought by Othniel (Judg. 3:7-11). With the establishment of the Israelite monarchy and also the establishment of the Aramean states to the northeast of her, there was automatically a clash of interests.[22]

Saul warred against the Aramean kingdom (I Sam. 14:47), but no names are given. David successfully fought with Hadadezer (Hadarezer – KJV: I Chron. 18:3, 5, 7; II Sam. 10:16-19), the son of Rehob, king of Zobah (likely in the area of Baalbek), and with his allies the Syrians of Damascus. Afterward David garrisoned the area (II Sam. 8:3 ff.; I Chron. 18:3 ff.). Over his victory David received the congratulations of Toi (Tou: I Chron. 18:9), king of Hamath, conveyed by his son Joram (II Sam. 8:9 ff.; Hadoram: I Chron. 18:9).

In a second round, at Helam, David fought with Hadadezer, who had at this time brought into the conflict the Arameans from beyond the river and whose commander was Shobach. Shobach was killed, but Hadadezer made peace with and became subject to Israel (II Sam. 10:15-18).[23]

Rezon, the son of Eliada, fled from his master Hadadezer, and following the slaughter of the army by David, he became the leader of a marauding band. The group came to dwell in Damascus where Rezon was made king and was an adversary

---

22 A. Malamat, "The Kingdom of David and Solomon in its Contact with Egypt and Aram Naharaim," *BA*, XXI (1958), 96 ff.; B. Mazar, "The Aramean Empire and its Relations with Israel," *BA*, XXV (1962), 98-120.

23 A. Noordtzij, "2 Samuel 8, 3-6," *ZAW*, XXVII (1907), 16 ff.

of Solomon throughout Solomon's reign (I Kings 11:23-25). It was conjectured by Kraeling that "Rezon" (LXX: 11:23 has "Ezron") is a corruption from "Hezion" and that Hezion was the first king of Damascus.[24] The case cannot be established, but Hezion appears again in the genealogy of Ben-hadad (I Kings 15:18).

David's political marriages brought him Ma'acah, the daughter of Talmai, king of Geshur (II Sam. 3:3). Later Absalom, as an exile, found sanctuary in the territory of this king, his grandfather, who was the son of Ammihud (II Sam. 13:37).

Much later, in the days of Elisha, a Syrian captain, Naaman, became the recipient of the wonder-working activities of that prophet (II Kings 5).

We have no external sources of information contemporary with the reign of David. Later Assyrian sources may imply an expansion of Aramean authority at this period, but the name of the Aramean king is not given.[25]

Ben-hadad I

Ben-hadad, son of Tabrimmon, the son of Hezion, was a contemporary of the Israelite kings Asa of Judah and Baasha of Israel (I Kings 15:16-18) ca. 909-885 B.C. In a conflict of these two kings with each other (ca. 879 B.C.) Asa used the treasures of the temple to hire Ben-hadad to break his league with Baasha, for which policy Asa was denounced by the seer Hanani (II Chron. 16:7-10). Ben-hadad proceeded to occupy Ijon, Dan, Abel-beth-ma'acah with all the land of Naphtali (I Kings 15: 20; II Chron. 16:4 ff.). It was likely he who established bazaars for Aramean merchants in Samaria (I Kings 20:34). A prolonged round of conflicts with Israel followed (cf. I Kings 20; 22).

A votive stele which now is in the possession of the Aleppo Museum was discovered in 1939 in a cemetery at Breidj about four miles north of Aleppo, which stele had been erected by Ben-hadad and dedicated to the god Melqart. It was published by Maurice Dunand the excavator of Byblos in 1941.[26] The

---

24 E. G. H. Kraeling, *Aram and Israel* (New York: Columbia University Press, 1918), p. 48.

25 Malamat, *op. cit.*, 96-102.

26 "Stèle araméene dediée à Melqart," *Bulletin du Musée de Beyrouth*, III (1939), 65-76; VI (1942-1943), 41-45. Cf. R. de Vaux, "Les prophètes de Baal sur le Mont Carmel," *Bulletin du Musée de Beyrouth*, V (1941), 9.

Aramaic inscription, conjecturally dated about 850 B.C., reads:

> A stele set up by Barhadad, the son of T[abrimmon, the son of Hezion], king of Aram, for his lord Melqart, which he vowed to him and he (then) heard his voice.[27]

On the stele the likeness of Melqart may be seen attired in a Syrian loin cloth and bearing a battleaxe and a composite bow, depicting the warlike character of the deity.

It is to be noticed that there are three Biblical names (cf. I Kings 15:18) in their Aramaic form on this stele if the reconstruction is accurate: Ben-hadad (Barhadad), Tabrimmon, and Hezion, giving the same line of succession as the Book of Kings does.

The question of how many figures there are in the Old Testament named Ben-hadad is a problem of long standing. Albright argues that the stele is evidence that the Ben-hadad of Asa's time is the same as that of Ahab's time (I Kings 20); thereby there are only two figures: Ben-hadad I and Ben-hadad II.[28] The case involves shortening the years allotted to Ben-hadad's reign to thirty-six years (879-843 B.C.) and construing the term "thy father" who had prior dealings with the Arameans (I Kings 20:34) in the sense of "predecessor."[29] Mazar takes the opposite position from Albright and argues that the Melqart stele refers to Ben-hadad II.[30] W. W. Hallo argues for three figures named Ben-hadad and leaves the question open as to which one this stele refers.[31]

Under the name Adad-'idri (Hadadezer) Ben-hadad is likely mentioned on the stele of Shalmaneser III as having opposed the Assyrians at the battle of Qarqar. For this battle he is said to have supplied 1,200 chariots, 1,200 cavalrymen, and 20,000 foot soldiers.[32]

---

27 ANET, p. 655.

28 W. F. Albright, "A Votive Stele Erected by Ben-Hadad I of Damascus to the God Melcarth," BASOR, No. 87 (1942), 23-29; G. Levi Della Vida and W. F. Albright, "Some Notes on the Stele of Ben-Hadad," BASOR, No. 90 (1943), 30-34; A. Jepsen, "Zur Melqart-Stele Barhadads," Archiv für Orientforschung, XVI (1952-1953), 315-317.

29 M. F. Unger, Israel and the Arameans of Damascus (London: James Clarke & Co., LTD, 1957), pp. 60-61.

30 Op. cit., 98-120.

31 "From Qarqar to Carchemish: Assyria and Israel in the Light of New Discoveries," BA, XXIII (1960), 39, n. 23.

32 ANET, p. 278. But cf. D. D. Luckenbill, "Benhadad and Hadadezer," AJSL, XXVII (1910(11)), 267-284; R. de Vaux, "La Chronologie de Hazael et de Benhadad III, rois de Damas," RB, XXXIV (1934), 512-518.

Ben-hadad (Adad-'idri) is further mentioned in accounts of a series of campaigns of Shalmaneser covering the sixth, tenth, eleventh, and fourteenth years of the latter's reign.[33] There is also an account of the demise of Ben-hadad and the rise of Hazael to the throne.

> I defeated Hadad-ezer of Damascus . . . Hadad-ezer (himself) perished. Hazael, a commoner (lit.: son of nobody), seized the throne.[34]

Hazael

Hazael's usurpation of the throne of Damascus (ca. 841-798 B.C.) was stimulated by the prophet Elisha (II Kings 8:7-15) when Hazael came to inquire concerning the chances of the recovery of his master, Ben-hadad. Hazael proceeded to murder Ben-hadad I (II?) by smothering him with a wet bed coverlet (II Kings 8:13-15). Somewhat earlier Elijah had been commissioned to designate him as successor to the throne (I Kings 19:15-18). Hazael began his conflicts with Israel by attacking Ramoth-gilead and seriously wounding Joram (II Kings 8:28-29). He continued to menace the Israelite kingdom through the reigns of Jehu (841-813 B.C.) and Jehoahaz (813-789 B.C.). Meanwhile he had taken possession of all Israelite territory in Trans-Jordan and Jehu was helpless to prevent the conquest (II Kings 10:32-33; Amos 1:3-4). Stretching himself beyond Israel into Philistia, he brought the downfall of Gath (II Kings 12:17). Only Jehoash's indemnity kept him from Jerusalem (II Kings 12:17-18; cf. II Chron. 24:23-24). In the north, eventually Jehoahaz's army was reduced by Hazael to a mere token force, and the oppression continued all of Jehoahaz's days (II Kings 13:17, 22). Hazael was succeeded on the throne by his son Ben-hadad (II Kings 15:24), but considerably later these earlier exchanges brought forth an oracle from the prophet Amos which threatened the doom of the house of Hazael (Amos 1:4).

Assyrian records refer to Hazael's usurpation as an act of "the son of a nobody":

> Hazael, a commoner (lit.: a son of nobody), seized the throne, called up a numerous army and rose against me. I fought with him and defeated him, taking the *chariots* of his camp. He disappeared to save his life. I marched as far as Damascus

---

33 *ANET*, pp. 279-280.
34 *Ibid.*, p. 280.

(*Di-ma-as-qi*), his royal residence [and cut down his] gardens.[35]

Hazael's name also occurs on a pavement slab from Nimrud where Shalmaneser reported attacking him in 841 B.C.,[36] in a fragment of an annalistic text,[37] on face B of the Black Obelisk describing a conflict of 837 B.C.,[38] and in an inscription from a marble bead.[39]

In the excavation of Arslan Tash (ancient *Hadatû*) in 1939 a piece of ivory, found with the remains of an ivory couch, came to light inscribed as "belonging to our Lord Hazael."[40] Also a figure on ivory from the same site has been conjectured by A. Parrot to be Hazael.[41] In the absence of further evidence, the conjecture cannot be made certain.

Hazael was succeeded on the throne of Damascus by his son Ben-hadad II (III?) (II Kings 13:24). This succession is mentioned in the Aramaic Zakir Inscription (lines 4 and 5), now in the Louvre,[42] which was found in 1904 twenty-five miles southeast of Aleppo at a place called Afis. On the stele Zakir, king of Hamath, recounts a deliverance for which he gives his gods credit. The danger came from a coalition with Ben-hadad at its head:

> Barhadad, the son of Hazael, king of Aram, united [seven of] a group of ten kings against me . . .[43]

Josephus reports that in his time (A.D. 37-100) Hazael and Ben-hadad were worshipped in Damascus because of their benefactions to the city:

> Then he took over the royal power himself, being a man of action and in great favour with the Syrians and the people of Damascus, by whom Adados and Azaelos who ruled after him are to this day honoured as gods because of their benefactions and the building of temples with which they adorned the city

35 *Ibid.*
36 *ARAB*, I, No. 663.
37 *ANET*, p. 280.
38 *Ibid.*
39 *Ibid.*, p. 281.
40 F. Thureau-Dangin, *Arslan Tash* (Paris: Paul Geuthner, 1931), p. 135.
41 *Samaria* (London: S.C.M. Press, 1958), pp. 40-41.
42 H. Pognon, *Inscriptions sémitiques de la Syrie, de la Mésopotamie et de la région de Mossoul* (Paris: Impr. nationale; Librairie V. Lecoffre, J. Gabalda, 1907), pp. 156-178, pls. ix, x, xxxv, xxxvi.
43 *ANET*, p. 655.

of Damascus. And they have processions every day in honour of these kings and glory in their antiquity, not knowing that these kings are rather recent and lived less than eleven hundred years ago.[44]

There is no confirming evidence for this claim.

It has been conjectured by Kraeling on the basis that "Mar" means "lord" that Mari, king of Damascus, who paid tribute to Adad-nirari, must be Ben-hadad;[45] but Unger argues that it is probably Hazael.[46] We have seen the title applied to him on the Arslan Tash ivory.

Ben-hadad II

Sometime about 801 B.C. Ben-hadad II (or III?), son of Hazael, succeeded his father on the throne of Damascus (II Kings 13:24). Ben-hadad, during the earlier part of the reign of Jehoash, continued to dominate Israel as his father Hazael had done (II Kings 13:3). But after this time Jehoash in three successive victories succeeded in recapturing the cities which Aram had taken from his father Jehoahaz (II Kings 13:24-25). The prophet Amos in his oracle against Damascus threatened the palace of Ben-hadad (Amos 1:4).

We meet this Ben-hadad on the Zakir inscription described earlier where Zakir, king of Hamath, relates that:

Barhadad the son of Hazael, king of Aram united [seven of] a group of ten kings against me: Barhadad and his army. . . .[47]

It is proposed by Stephanie Page that the tribute from "Mari' of the land of Damascus" claimed by Adad-nirari III on the Tell al Rimah stele might either be that of Hazael or of Ben-hadad, his son, but that it is more likely from Ben-hadad. Page argues that since it is known from the Arslan Tash ivory that "Lord (Mar)" was applied to Hazael, it is also likely that it was worn by his son.[48] Joash seems to have seized this moment to send tribute to Assyria and recover the lands his predecessor had lost to Hazael.

---

44 *Ant.* ix. 4. 6 (93-94).
45 *Op. cit.*, p. 83; cf. D. D. Luckenbill, *ARAB*, I, Nos. 734 f.
46 *Op. cit.*, p. 83.
47 *ANET*, p. 655; cf. J. Lewy, "Studies in the Historic Geography of the Ancient Near East," *Orientalia*, XXI (1952), 418 ff.; M. Noth, "La^cash und Hazrak," *ZDPV*, LII (1929), 124-141.
48 "A Stela of Adad-Nirari III and Nergal-Eres from Tell al Rimah," *Iraq*, XXX (1968), 149-150.

Rezin

Laying aside past quarrels between Israel and Aram, Rezin, king of Syria *ca.* 750-732 B.C., formed an alliance with Pekah, king of Israel, against Ahaz, king of Judah (II Kings 15:37). These two kings about 735 B.C. besieged Ahaz, but could not conquer him (II Kings 16:5; Isa. 7:1). At the news of the alliance the young king Ahaz was frightened: "His heart shook as trees of the forest shake before the wind" (Isa. 7:2). Also his people melted in fear (Isa. 8:6). Pekah and Rezin planned to displace Ahaz with "the son of Tabeel" (Isa. 7:6). Against the advice of Isaiah, who called the two kings "two smoldering stumps of firebrands" (Isa. 7:4), Ahaz with the temple treasure, hired Tiglath-pileser III to attack Israel and Damascus. Ahaz was thereby delivered from the danger, but portions of the northern kingdom were taken into exile (II Kings 15:29). Tiglath-pileser also at this time (*ca.* 732 B.C.) took Damascus, carried its people captive to Kir, and killed Rezin (II Kings 16:9).

In the same cuneiform text of an unknown year in which Menahem of Judah is listed as tributary, Tiglath-pileser III also lists Rezin:

> I received tribute from Kushtashpi of Commagene (*Kummuhu*), Rezon (*Ra-hi-a-nu*) of Damascus (*Sa-imerisu*)....[49]

Although the records of Tiglath-pileser that deal with the end of Damascus are fragmentary and mutilated, a section of the annals assumed to refer to the fall of Damascus relates that Rezin fled the city, his chief advisers were impaled, and the gardens were ravaged.[50]

Also in a record of events after the ninth year of his reign (743 B.C.) Tiglath-pileser records:

> I laid siege to and captured the town of Hadara, the inherited property of Rezon of Damascus (*Sa-imerisu*) [the place where] he was born. I brought away as prisoners 800 (of its) inhabitants with their possessions, . . . their large (and) small cattle, 750 prisoners from Kurussa [. . . prisoners] from Irma, 550 prisoners from Metuna I brought (also) away. 502 towns . . . of the 16 districts of the country of Damascus (*Sa-imerisu*) I destroyed (making them look) like the hills of (ruined) cities over which the flood (had swept).[51]

---

49 *ANET*, p. 283.
50 *ARAB*, I, No. 776.
51 *ANET*, p. 283.

There formerly existed an Assyrian record of Rezin's death which, after it has been read by Rawlinson, was lost.[52]

SUMMARY

From the neighbors in close proximity to Israel we have gleaned a total of five names about which archaeological discovery has furnished us records in which their names occur. Josephus has transmitted the record of Menander on two others: Hiram and Ithbaal. From archaeology there is one Moabite — Mesha — and four Arameans: Ben-hadad I, Hazael, Ben-hadad II, and Rezin. Contrary to what might seem the normal expectation, to this point, this area proves to be one of the lesser known areas of Old Testament studies.

---

52 E. Schrader, *The Cuneiform Inscriptions and the Old Testament*, trans. by O. C. Whitehouse (London: Williams and Norgate, 1885), I, 252, 257.

IV

GOD'S SERVANTS

The vacuum left in the Middle East by the demise of Assyria was quickly filled by Babylon who for some time had been asserting her independence. She had joined with the Scythians and the Medes to bring an end to Nineveh in 612 B.C. and then proceeded to checkmate Egyptian ambitions of expansion by defeating Necho at Carchemish in 605 B.C.

Our first figure from the Babylonian region antedates the fall of Nineveh by a century, first appears on the scene of history in the time of Tiglath-pileser III, and is the first Babylonian ruler to be mentioned by name in the Hebrew Bible.

MERODACH-BALADAN

Merodach-baladan, son of Baladan, king of Babylon, sent envoys to Hezekiah when he had heard that the latter had recovered from his illness. Hezekiah received the envoys kindly and showed them all his treasures and his storehouses. When Isaiah inquired of their identity and of what they had seen, the king confessed that they were from Babylon and that they had seen all. The prophet told Hezekiah that days would come when all that was in his house would be taken to Babylon and that some of his sons would be eunuchs in the palace of the king of Babylon. Hezekiah could merely reply: "The word you have spoken is good," for he thought, "There will be peace and security in my days" (Isa. 39:1-8; cf. II Kings 20:12-19).

The writer of Chronicles, without mentioning Merodach-baladan by name, suggests that the envoys came to inquire about the sign that had been done in the land (II Chron. 32:31). Josephus gives yet a third motive for their coming which, if true,

73

explains the adverse view which Isaiah took of Hezekiah's relations with them:

> Now it happened at this time that the empire of the Assyrians was destroyed by the Medes, but I shall write of this in another place. And the king of Babylon named Baladas, sent envoys bearing gifts to Hezekiah and invited them to become his ally and friend. Thereupon he gladly received the envoys and feasted them.[1]

Merodach-baladan of the tribe of Bit-Jakin first appears in history in the royal inscriptions of Tiglath-pileser III and in the Nimrud letters.[2] He is mentioned by name in at least three of these letters (letters V, IX, and LXV). This sparse material is further supplemented by the *Babylonian Chronicle*. From these sources it can be deduced that the chieftain (dignified by the Assyrians with the title of "king") made his submission to Tiglath-pileser. Later, in 722 B.C., during the uncertainties that characterized the early days of Sargon II's reign, Merodach-baladan assumed the reign of Babylon for which post he claims that he was hand picked by Marduk, god of Babylon. Sargon's records, on the other hand, allude to him as a "foreigner" though indeed he was a Chaldean. Merodach-baladan's rule is documented in Babylon, Borsippa, Cutha, Kish, Nippur, Sippar, Ur, and Uruk.

When, after a dozen years, Sargon was free to deal with the problem, Merodach-baladan's territory was overrun and his fortress, Dur-Jakin, was taken. Sargon established his own rule over Babylon in 709 B.C. Many people of Dur-Jakin were deported and no more of Merodach-baladan is heard during Sargon's reign. Under Sennacherib he was again ruling in Babylon about 703 B.C. after he had removed the Assyrian puppet. He stirred up the Assyrian vassals in the West to rebel and it is likely to this end that he sent his envoys to Hezekiah. Sennacherib promptly took Babylon, but Merodach-baladan retreated into his homeland and found refuge in Elam about 700 B.C. from

---

1 Josephus *Ant.* x. 2. 2 (30 ff.). The variant spellings Berodach-baladan (II Kings 20:12) and Merodach-baladan (Isa. 39:1) are explained by some scholars upon the basis of variation in pronunciation of the "B" and "M" sounds in Akkadian. Others argue that the variant is a scribal error due to early Hebrew epigraphy.

2 R. W. Rogers, *Cuneiform Parallels to the Old Testament* (New York: Abingdon Press, 1926), pp. 210 ff. For a summary of information on Merodach-baladan, see J. A. Brinkman, "Merodach-baladan II," in *Studies Presented to H. Leo Oppenheim* (Chicago: The Oriental Institute of the University of Chicago, 1964), pp. 6-53.

whence he continued to carry on intrigues. Some years later in 691 B.C. his son Nabu-suma-iskun was taken captive by Sennacherib, but other relatives continued to make trouble for the Assyrians.

In addition to the types of records mentioned above, Merodach-baladan's name occurs in Sargonic letters, twice in King List A with reigns of twelve years and nine months respectively, in a colophon to a late list of plants, and in six "slave documents," dating from the ninth to the twelfth years of his reign. Furthermore, M. E. Mallowan found a cylinder in three pieces at Nimrud inscribed to his order telling how the Assyrians had been driven out of Akkad. This discovery demonstrates that

12. BOUNDARY STONE DEPICTING MERODACH-BALADAN (left) and an official. Courtesy, Staatliche Museen zu Berlin

Merodach-baladan was a thorn in the flesh to four successive Assyrian kings beginning with Tiglath-pileser III and ending with Sennacherib.[3]

A number of years ago the Berlin Museum purchased a boundary stone (kudurru) (VA 2663) of black marble of about 46 cm. height whose inscription identified the form it depicts as: "Image of Marduk-apla-iddina, King of Babylon." Standing to the left is the king wearing a long skirt with slipper-like shoes and a pointed cap and holding a staff in his left hand and an unidentified object in his right hand. He is presenting an official, Belakhkhe-eriba, with a piece of land "for ever." It is assumed that the other figure on the monument in smaller stature is this official.[4]

NEBUCHADNEZZAR

No non-Jewish monarch occupies more space in the Bible than does Nebuchadnezzar, whose chief role is that of the exiler of Judah in 597 B.C. and again in 586 B.C. His name appears in the Bible more than ninety times in the alternate spellings Nebuchadnezzar (II Kings 24:1; etc.) and Nebuchadrezzar (Jer. 43: 10 ff.; etc.). In addition to his prominence in the canonical books, he is also noticed in the Apocrypha in I Esdras, in the additions to Esther, in Baruch, Judith, and Tobit. As is to be expected he also occupies a very prominent place in rabbinic literature among the enemies of God's people.

Necho's defeat at Carchemish at the hands of Nebuchadnezzar is the subject of an oracle of Jeremiah. The event is dated in the fourth year of Jehoiachim (Jer. 46:2 ff.). Also an undated oracle collected in the same context deals with his smiting of the land of Egypt (Jer. 46:13 ff.).

The book of Daniel attributes to Nebuchadnezzar a siege of Jerusalem in the third year of Jehoiachim at which time some vessels of the temple, some of the royal family, some of the nobility, and some youths of the royal family were carried to Babylon. Among the captives were Daniel and his companions who were later called Shadrach, Meshach, and Abednego (Dan. 1:1-7).

Following vassalage to Egypt during the years 609-605 B.C., Je-

---

3 *Nimrud and Its Remains* (London: Collins, 1966), I, 174-175; C. J. Gadd, "Inscribed Barrel Cylinder of Marduk-apla-iddina II," *Iraq*, XV (1953), 123-134.

4 *ANEP*, No. 454; Eva Strommenger, *The Art of Mesopotamia* (London: Thames and Hudson, 1964), p. 457.

13. BABYLONIAN BRICK stamped with the names of Nabopolassar, founder of the Neo-Babylonian Empire and his son Nebuchadnezzar whose armies took Israel into exile. Courtesy, British Museum

hoiachim became vassal to Nebuchadnezzar who had also taken all the territory formerly belonging to Egypt from the Brook of Egypt to the river Euphrates (II Kings 24:7). The Book of Chronicles, in an episode unparalleled in Kings, relates that Nebuchadnezzar bound Jehoiachim in fetters to take him to Babylon and also carried away part of the vessels of the temple to his palace in Babylon (II Chron. 36:6-7).

After three years' vassalage Jehoiachim revolted (II Kings 24: 1) and brought down the wrath of Nebuchadnezzar upon himself, but before the fall of Jerusalem, he was succeeded on the throne by his son Jehoiachin. The circumstances of Jehoiachim's death are not clear to us. Josephus reports that Nebuchadnezzar

slew him and cast his body unburied before the walls.[5] Jehoiachin, the new king, capitulated (II Kings 24:10 ff.). Not only
the royal family and officials, but also ten thousand men of valor
and the smiths and craftsmen, were exiled (II Kings 24:14;
cf. v. 16; Esther 2:6). The treasures of the temple and of the
king's house were also carried off (II Kings 24:12-13).

In the years which followed, Jeremiah, in his vision of the
baskets of figs, found in these exiles in Babylon the future hope
of the nation rather than in those people who had remained in
Jerusalem (Jer. 24:1 ff.). He advised them to attempt a normal
life in their exile home (Jer. 29:1 ff.). Each of these events is
introduced to us as having taken place after Jehoiachin and his
family were carried off (cf. I Chron. 6:15).

Following the capitulation of Jehoiachin, the king of Babylon
put upon the throne Mattaniah, a third son of Josiah, whose
name he changed to Zedekiah. At the beginning of this reign
Jeremiah announced that Babylonian domination was to be for
at least three generations (Jer. 27:7). When further confronted
with the unrest created by Hananiah, who insisted that the cap-
tivity would last only two years, Jeremiah insisted that the cap-
tivity would be long and that the Lord had put the neck of the
nations into a yoke of servitude to Nebuchadnezzar (Jer. 28:
1 ff.). Those prophets who continued to stir the people to revolt
would be delivered into his hands to be slain (Jer. 29:21).
However, after a time Zedekiah also was drawn into revolt;
consequently, in the tenth month of the ninth year of his reign,
Nebuchadnezzar again came west to besiege Jerusalem (II
Kings 24:17—25:1; Jer. 39:1; 52:4 ff.). In the face of Zedekiah's
vacillating policy, Jeremiah was adamant in his insistency that
Jerusalem would be delivered into the hands of Nebuchadnezzar (Jer. 32:28). After an extended siege lasting until the eleventh year and the fourth month, the wall of Jerusalem was
breached. Though he escaped from the city by night, Zedekiah, along with his officials, was captured at Jericho and taken
into Nebuchadnezzar's presence at Riblah on the Orontes. There
his sons were killed and Zedekiah himself was blinded before
being taken in fetters to Babylon (Jer. 39:1-6; II Kings 25:2-7).

Nebuchadnezzar's captain, Nebuzaradan, burned the temple,
the palace, and every great house in Jerusalem and destroyed
the walls of the city. Significant figures were executed, but exiles
were again taken to Babylon. A special charge had been given

_____

5 *Ant.* x. 6. 3 (97).

by Nebuchadnezzar concerning Jeremiah which gave him an option, and he elected to remain in Palestine (Jer. 39:11-14; 40:1-6). Bronze, gold, and silver vessels were carried off (II Kings 25:8 ff.; Jer. 52:12 ff.).[6] At least some of the vessels carried off are said later to have been used by Belshazzar in his great feast (Dan. 5:2). Still later, some were restored to Jerusalem by Cyrus at the end of the exile (Ezra 1:7; 5:14; 6: 5). Some of the exiles who returned under the leadership of Zerubbabel are identified as being connected with Nebuchadnezzar's exile (Neh. 7:6).

Gedaliah, son of Ahikam, son of Shaphan, was now designated governor in Judah to rule those people left in the land. Gedaliah established his seat of government at Mizpah (II Kings 25:22 ff.). After an unknown lapse of time, in the seventh month of the year, he was murdered by Ishmael and his associates (II Kings 25:25; cf. Jer. 39:14).

In addition to his part in the downfall of the Jewish state, Nebuchadnezzar comes to notice in an oracle of Jeremiah concerning "Kedar and the Kingdom of Hazor" (Jer. 49:28 ff.). After being taken to Egypt, at Tahpanhes, Jeremiah also predicted an Egyptian invasion by Nebuchadnezzar (Jer. 43:10). Despite the significant role played by the king in the thought of the prophet as God's servant (Jer. 25:9; 27:6; 43:10), he threatened that God would bring punishment upon him for his treatment of Judah (Jer. 50:17-18).

The prophet Ezekiel in an oracle dated in the eleventh year (586 B.C.) threatened Tyre with an invasion by Nebuchadnezzar (Ezek. 26:7 ff.). At a later date, the twenty-seventh year (571 B.C.), he promised Egypt to Nebuchadnezzar for the lack of gain acquired in the long siege of Tyre (Ezek. 29:17-20). Josephus describes this siege as lasting thirteen years.[7] Yet again Ezekiel threatened Egypt with prospective invasion by Nebuchadnezzar (Ezek. 30:10 ff.).

Nebuchadnezzar's dream of the great image, dated in the second year of his reign, is the theme of Chapter 2 of Daniel. The story of the great image set up by Nebuchadnezzar in the plain of Dura, which Daniel's companions refused to worship, is related in Chapter 3. Nebuchadnezzar's insanity is related in Chapter 4. In the course of this last narrative Nebuchadnezzar's role as builder of Babylon is noticed:

6 *Ibid.*, x. 9. 1 (155 ff.).
7 *Against Apion* i. 21 (156).

14. NEBUCHADNEZZAR'S BABYLON as reconstructed on the basis of archaeological discovery. Courtesy, Oriental Institute

"Is this not great Babylon, which I have built by my mighty power as a royal residence and for the glory of my majesty?" (Dan. 4:30).

Finally, a cross reference to the greatness of Nebuchadnezzar's rule and to his insanity is made in the course of interpreting to Belshazzar the handwriting on the wall (Dan. 5:18). Nebuchadnezzar's building activities in Babylon are amply attested both in cuneiform sources and by excavation. A brick in the British Museum (BM 90081) gives his name and titles and records his restoration of the temples Esagila and Ezida at Babylon, sacred to the gods Marduk and Nabu.[8] Josephus records his adorning of the temple of Bel and his making the hanging gardens to please his queen who was from Media.[9] He built and left his record on the Great Procession Way along which Marduk passed in the festival of the New Year:

> Nebuchadnezzar, king of Babylon, . . . son of Nabopolassar, king of Babylon, am I. In Aibursabum the street of Babylon, for the triumphal procession of my great lord Marduk a bridge for the canal I constructed and its course I widened. Oh, Marduk, great lord, . . . grant enduring life. . . .[10]

Elsewhere he describes other building works:

> When Marduk the great lord created me the legitimate son and to direct the affairs of the land, to shepherd the people, to care for the city, to rebuild the temples, sent me in his great power, I was tremblingly obedient unto Marduk my lord. For Babylon his mighty city, the city of his supreme power, Imgur-Bel and Nimitti-Bel, its great walls I completed. Upon the thresholds of their great gates strong bulls of bronze, and terrible serpents standing upright, I placed. That which no previous king had done, my father did in that he put about the city with mortar and brick two of its moat walls. As for me, a third great moat wall, one against the second I built with mortar and brick, and, with the moat-wall of my father joined and closely united it. Its foundation upon the bosom of the abyss I laid down deeply, its top I raised mountain high.
> A moat-wall of burnt brick to the west of the wall of Babylon I placed about the city.
> The moat-walls of the canal Araḫtu my father built securely

8 D. J. Wiseman, *Illustrations from Biblical Archaeology* (London: Tyndale Press, 1958), p. 71.

9 *Ant.* x. 11. 1 (224-226).

10 Stephen Langdon, *Building Inscriptions of the Neo-Babylonian Empire* (Paris: Ernest LeRoux, 1905), pp. 81-83.

with mortar and burnt brick, quays of burnt brick along the
farther side of the Euphrates he laid securely but did not finish all the work. As for me his first-born son, the beloved of
his heart, the moat-walls of Araḫtu I built with mortar and
burnt brick, and joined them with those of my father, making
them very solid.

In Esagila, the awe-inspiring house, palace of heaven and
earth, abode of joy, Ekua, the shrine of the lord of the gods
Marduk, Ka-ḫili-sug, the abode of Zarpanit, Ezida, the abode
of the king of the gods of heaven and earth, with shining gold
I clothed and made to shine as daylight. Etemin-anki, the
zikkurrat of Babylon, I rebuilt. Ezida, the faithful house beloved of Nebo, I rebuilt in Barsippa, with gold and jewels I
built it like the scenery of heaven.[11]

The excavations of R. Koldeway on the site of Babylon (1899-
1917) chiefly revealed remains of the period of Nebuchadnezzar II (604-562 B.C.).[12] Babylon's ziggurat (temple tower)
mentioned in the quotation above is described by Herodotus.[13]
Various business texts are extant which are dated by Nebuchadnezzar's years.[14] He left inscriptions at Nahr el-Kelb, north
of Beirut, and in Wadi Brissa on the road to Hamath.[15]

Until the second quarter of this century historical texts from
Nebuchadnezzar's reign covering his military activities were
lacking, and it was only in 1956 that the most important of them
was published.[16] This Babylonian Chronicle gives information
making possible a reconstruction of events and dates of the
first ten years of his reign. As did the Assyrian kings, he carried on numerous campaigns and dealt brutally with defeated
enemies. Numerous campaigns were directed against the Syro-
Palestinian areas. Out of his records the most exciting are his
descriptions of the battle of Carchemish and of the capture at a

---

11 Langdon, op. cit., pp. 61-63.
12 The Excavations at Babylon, trans. by A. S. Johns (London: Macmillan and Co., 1914), 335 pp.
13 Histories i. 181.
14 Collections of these documents are to be found in Ellen Whitley
Moore, Neo-Babylonian Documents in the University of Michigan Collection (Ann Arbor: University of Michigan Press, 1939; in Raymond Philip
Dougherty, Archives from Erech, Time of Nebuchadrezzar and Nabonidus
(Goucher College Cuneiform Inscriptions, Vol. I, New Haven: Yale University Press, 1923) and Archives from Erech, Neo-Babylonian and Persian Periods (Goucher College Cuneiform Inscriptions, Vol. II, New Haven:
Yale University Press, 1933).
15 ANET, p. 307.
16 D. J. Wiseman, Chronicles of Chaldean Kings (London: British
Museum, 1956), 99 pp.

later time of Jerusalem, March 15/16, 597 B.C., in the time of Jehoiachin.

Nebuchadnezzar's role in the battle of Carchemish as leader of the army, though still only crown prince, is surveyed by both Josephus,[17] who claims Berossos as his source of information, and also by the *Babylonian Chronicle*[18] — the only two non-Biblical sources of information on this important event. Though the Neo-Babylonian empire was founded by Nabopolassar, he entrusted the checkmating of Egyptian expansion to crown prince Nebuchadnezzar. Nebuchadnezzar won victory over Necho at Carchemish in 605 B.C. and proceeded to take over all Egyptian holdings east of the river of Egypt (Wadi el 'Arish). Also Nebuchadnezzar's speedy return to Babylon following the death of his father is recounted in the same above mentioned two sources.[19] In Babylon he ascended the throne September 6/7, 605 B.C.,[20] and in that year carried out a campaign in Syria lasting until February, 604 B.C.[21] In another campaign the next year it is claimed that "all the kings of Hatti came before Nebuchadnezzar."[22] Jehoiachim is not mentioned in the *Chronicle*, but it is likely that his submission (II Kings 24:1) came at this time along with that of the other kings. Among several other campaigns in succeeding years one is against Askelon. At approximately this time a Palestinian king called Adon wrote to Pharaoh requesting aid in the face of the Babylonian king.[23] In 601 B.C. Nebuchadnezzar in a battle with Egypt suffered a severe set back.[24] Josephus recounts a payment of tribute (not related in the Bible) by Jehoiachim in the fourth year of Nebuchadnezzar.[25]

The campaign of 598/7 B.C. was directed against Jerusalem. According to Josephus, Jehoiachim vainly had expected a Baby-

---

17 *Against Apion* i. 19 (132); *Ant.* x. 6. 1 (84-86).
18 Wiseman, *Chronicles of Chaldean Kings,* pp. 67-69.
19 Josephus *Against Apion,* i. 19 (136-138); Wiseman, *Chronicles of Chaldean Kings,* pp. 25-27, 69.
20 Wiseman, *Chronicles of Chaldean Kings,* p. 27.
21 *Ibid.*
22 *Ibid.,* p. 28.
23 D. W. Thomas, *Documents from Old Testament Times* (Edinburgh and London: Thomas Nelson and Sons Ltd., 1958), pp. 251 ff.; Wiseman, *Chronicles of Chaldean Kings,* p. 28, n. 5; J. A. Fitzmyer, "The Aramaic Letters of King Adon to the Egyptian Pharaoh," *Biblica,* XLVI (1965), 41 ff.
24 Wiseman, *Chronicles of Chaldean Kings,* p. 29.
25 *Ant.* x. 6. 1 (87); cf. Wiseman, *Chronicles of Chaldean Kings,* pp. 30-31.

lonian-Egyptian conflict and ceased to pay his tribute.[26] The king and his army left Babylon in December, 598, and captured Jerusalem by mid-March. The *Chronicle* states tersely:

> In the seventh year, the month of Kislev, the king of
> Akkad mustered his troops, marched to Hatti-land,
> and encamped against (*i.e.*, besieged) the city of Judah
> and on the second day of the month of Adar he seized
> the city and captured the king.
> He appointed there a king of his own choice (lit. heart),
> received its heavy tribute and sent (them) to Babylon.[27]

This text sets precisely the date for the fall of Jerusalem as March 15/16, 597 B.C., and is one of the most exciting and specific contacts between archaeological information and Biblical information. No names of the Judean kings involved in the exchange are given in the *Chronicle*. Unfortunately, it does not deal with the campaign against Zedekiah in 586 B.C. and the final downfall of Jerusalem; consequently, we have no Babylonian record of that event.

Questions of long standing in Biblical studies are Nebuchadnezzar's campaigns against Tyre and Egypt. Josephus claims Philostratos' *History of Phoenicia* as his authority for his assertion that Nebuchadnezzar besieged Tyre for thirteen years when Ithobalos was king of Tyre.[28] Elsewhere Josephus also gives the same information merely as excerpted from "the Phoenician records."[29] The extant *Babylonian Chronicle* does not cover the period of this event, but that Tyre fell to Nebuchadnezzar seems established from the combined evidence of a cuneiform tablet which refers to provisions "for the king and the troops which have gone with him to the land of Tyre"; of an official document which includes the king of Tyre among Babylonian officials; and of a business document which mentions the Babylonian commissioner of Tyre.[30]

---

26 *Ant.* x. 6. 2 (88-89).

27 Wiseman, *Chronicles of Chaldean Kings*, p. 73, 11. 11-13; D. N. Freedman, "The Babylonian Chronicle," *BA*, XIX (1956), 50-60; J. P. Hyatt, "New Light on Nebuchadrezzar and Judean History," *JBL*, LXXV (1956), 277-284.

28 *Ant.* x. 11. 1 (228). Codex Laurentianus contains variant reading of "three years."

29 *Against Apion* i. 21 (156).

30 E. Unger, "Nebukadnezar II und sein Sandabakku (Oberkommisar) in Tyrus," *ZAW*, XLIV (1926), 314-317; W. F. Albright, "The Seal of Eliakim and the Latest Pre-exilic History of Judah, with some Observations on Ezekiel," *JBL*, LI (1932), 94, n. 48.

Even more sparse is information on the invasion of Egypt. Josephus, after recounting the flight of Jews into Egypt following the murder of Gedaliah, relates that Nebuchadnezzar "invaded Egypt in order to subdue it, and having killed the king who was then reigning and appointed another, he again took captive the Jews who were in the country and carried them to Babylon."[31] The *Babylonian Chronicle* again does not cover the relevant years, but according to a broken religious text now in the British Museum (BM 33041, 33053), Nebuchadnezzar in his thirty-seventh year (568/7 B.C.) carried out a campaign in Egypt against Pharaoh Amasis. The city of Putu-Iaman is clearly mentioned as being involved.[32]

The death of Nebuchadnezzar and the succession to the throne of Evil-Merodach is recounted by Josephus, which information he maintains he found in Berossos.[33]

EVIL-MERODACH

Information on the period of the exile following the capitulation of Jerusalem is not abundant. One event, however, is reported in the experiences of Jehoiachin and gives a welcomed insight into the period. Evil-Merodach (562-560 B.C.), son of and successor to Nebuchadnezzar on the throne of Babylon, in the first year of his reign freed Jehoiachin, king of Judah, from prison (II Kings 25:27-30; Jer. 52:31-34). The date of this episode, the twenty-seventh of the twelfth month of the thirty-seventh year of Jehoiachin's exile (*i.e.* 562 B.C.), is the last date cited in the book of Kings. Jehoiachin put off his prison garments and was given a seat above the seats of the kings in Babylon with Evil-Merodach. For the remainder of his life a regular allowance was given him by the king, and he dined at the king's table every day as long as he lived. The date of Jehoiachin's death is unknown.

Unfortunately, no fragments of the *Babylonian Chronicle* cover the two years of this king's reign. His name in Akkadian is Awel-Marduk (man of Marduk). A basalt stele now in Istanbul, among other details of the rise to power of Nabonidus, reports:

---

31 *Ant.* x. 9. 7 (182).
32 Wiseman, *Chronicles of Chaldean Kings*, p. 94; *ANET*, p. 308; see also W. M. Flinders Petrie, *Tanis*, pt. 2: *Nebesheh (AM) and Defenneh (Tahpanhes)* (London: Trübner & Co., 1888), pp. 50-51.
33 *Against Apion* i. 20 (146); *Ant.* x. 11. 1, 2 (219, 229).

Awel-Marduk, son of Nebuchadnezzar, and Labashi-Marduk, son of Neri-glissar [called up] their [troo]ps and . . . their . . . they dispersed.[34]

A break then follows in the text.

Berossos, as cited by Josephus, listed Evilmaraduch (*sic.*) as son and successor to Nebuchadnezzar and stated that his government was arbitrary and licentious and that after a reign of two years he was assassinated by his sister's husband, Neriglissar:

After beginning the wall of which I have spoken, Nabuchodonosor fell sick and died, after a reign of forty-three years, and the realm passed to his son Evilmaraduch. This prince, whose government was arbitrary and licentious, fell a victim to a plot, being assassinated by his sister's husband, Neriglisar, after a reign of two years.[35]

NERGALSHAREZER

Nergalsharezer is mentioned in the Bible only in connection with the final destruction of Jerusalem by Nebuchadnezzar in 587 B.C. When Jerusalem had been taken, "all the princes of the king of Babylon came and sat in the middle gate: Nergal-sharezer, Samgar-nebo, Sarsechim the Rabsaris, Nergal-sharezer the Rabmag; with all the rest of the officers of the king of Babylon" (Jer. 39:3).

Nergal-shar-usur (559-556 B.C.), called Neriglissar in the Greek accounts, son of a private citizen Belsum-iskun, was son-in-law of Nebuchadnezzar and succeeded to the throne of Babylon for four years following the death of Awel-Marduk. Whether his accession was the result of a revolution or was the rise of the next male in the royal line of succession following the death of his brother-in-law is not clear.[36] Berossos states that Evil-Merodach was assassinated by Neriglissar.[37] Josephus, obviously in error (after having elsewhere cited Berossos), calls him Eglisaros, son of Abilmathadachos, and attributes to him a reign of forty years.[38]

Nergal-shar-usur's name occurs in contract tablets and in building inscriptions. He was a rich landowner with properties at Babylon and at Opis and was in control of the affairs of

---

34 *ANET*, p. 309.
35 *Against Apion* i. 20 (146-147).
36 Wiseman, *Chronicles of Chaldean Kings*, p. 38.
37 Josephus *Against Apion*, i. 20 (147-148).
38 *Ant.* x. 11. 2 (231).

the sun-god temple at Sippar. He also restored temples at Babylon and Borsippa.[39] The only historical text extant for his
reign is BM 25124. In his third year he led his army into Cilicia and executed a defeat on Appuasu by which means he, like
his predecessors, maintained a hold on East Cilicia.[40]
It is thought likely that this Babylonian figure is identical
with the prince mentioned in Jeremiah.

BELSHAZZAR

Belshazzar the king, last ruler of Babylon in the Book of Daniel, was once one of the most problematic figures of Biblical history. Events are dated from his first and third regnal years in
Daniel 7 and 8. His great feast for a thousand lords during
which he drank from the vessels brought away from the temple
in Jerusalem is considered by the author of Daniel to be the ul-
timate in sacrilege. The deciphering of the handwriting on the
wall, "Mene, Mene, Tekel, and Parsin," which the wise men could
not interpret, but which Daniel interpreted, has for all readers
of the Bible, rightly exalted the wisdom of Daniel. By convert-
ing the Aramaic nouns for weights into verbs and by expound-
ing the verbs (so it would seem) Daniel read: "God has num-
bered the days of your kingdom and brought it to an end. You
have been weighed in the balances and found wanting. Your
kingdom is divided and given to the Medes and Persians." The
interpretation brought rewards to Daniel and caused his elevation to the position of third ruler in the kingdom. That night,
however, brought death to Belshazzar the Chaldean and brought
an end to the Babylonian empire (Dan. 5).

Classical sources are silent on a rule of Belshazzer. Herodotus
merely says that the city of Babylon fell when Labynetus, son of
an older Labynetus and his queen, Nitocris, was king of Babylon.[41] Xenophon tells in detail of the fall of the city to Gobryas,
general of Cyrus, and tells of the slaughter of the young Babylonian king, but gives no name for him.[42]

The book of Baruch has Jews in Babylon to urge those in Palestine:

And pray for the life of Nebuchadnezzar king of Babylon,
and for the life of Belshazzar his son, that their days upon

39 Wiseman, *Chronicles of Chaldean Kings*, p. 38.
40 *Ibid.*, pp. 38-42; S. Langdon and R. Zehnpfund, *Die neubabylonischen Königsinschriften* (Vorderasiatische Bibliothek, IV; Leipzig: J. C. Hein-richs, 1912), pp. 277, 290.
41 *Histories* i. 188 ff.
42 *Cyropaedia* vii. 5. 29, 30.

the earth may be like the days of heaven. And the Lord will give us strength, and he will give light to our eyes, and we may live under the protection of Nebuchadnezzar king of Babylon, and under the protection of Belshazzar his son, and we shall serve them many days, and may find favor in their sight (Baruch 1:11, 12).

This source, of course, is not independent of the Bible.

Josephus in the *Antiquities* identified Belshazzar with Nabonidus: "It [the kingship] then passed to Baltasares, who was called Naboandelos by the Babylonians,"[43] but in *Against Apion* where he is summarizing Berossos, he did not mention Belshazzar.[44] Josephus assigned a seventeen year reign to Baltasaros and stated that he was the end of the posterity of Nebuchadnezzar.[45] One cannot know whether Josephus drew these additions to Scripture from sources or from his own mind.

With such confusing material at their disposal, little wonder that earlier scholars puzzled over the problem of Belshazzar!

Since Dougherty collected the available cuneiform evidence, the existence of Belshazzar is beyond dispute. Nothing like a biography exists, but a tablet in the Yale University collection dated in the accession year of Neriglissar refers to Belshazzar, the chief officer of the king. However, though this Belshazzar may be the Biblical figure, since his father's name is not given, one cannot be certain of the identity.[46]

Six texts, ranging from years one to fourteen of the reign of Nabonidus give information concerning some of the minor business aspects of Belshazzar's life. These business documents deal with sale of land and with loans of money by servants, scribes, or stewards of Belshazzar.[47] Six texts show that Belshazzar made gifts of gold, silver, and sacrificial animals to the Babylonian sanctuaries.[48]

The name of Belshazzar is clearly associated with that of Nabonidus in governmental matters. Four cylinders found in the ziggurat at Ur contain copies of a prayer of Nabonidus that includes "Belshazzar, the first son."[49] Also the same phrase is

---

43 x. 11. 2 (231).
44 i. 20 (149-151).
45 *Ant.* x. 11. 4 (247-248).
46 R. P. Dougherty, *Nabonidus and Belshazzar* (New Haven: Yale University Press, 1929), pp. 67-69.
47. *Ibid.*, pp. 81 ff.
48. *Ibid.*, p. 87.
49 *Ibid.*, p. 93.

twice in a variant of the prayer on a large cylinder of the same provenience.[50] Three other texts associate his name with that of Nabonidus in oath formulas.[51] Two occurrences are in an astrological report of the seventh year,[52] and one text gives the title of an official as: "Chief officer of Belshazzar, the son of the king."[53]

Nabonidus spent a good portion of his reign in Tema. During these years he left Belshazzar in charge in Babylon. The *Nabonidus Chronicle* for the seventh, ninth, and eleventh years reports: "The king stayed in Tema; the crown prince, the officials and the army were in Akkad."[54] The portion of the *Persian Verse Account* which is extant has neither the name of Nabonidus nor of Belshazzar, but the editor, Sidney Smith, argued convincingly that Nabonidus and Belshazzar are its subjects.[55] Here also Belshazzar is in charge:

> He entrusted the "Camp" to his oldest (son), the firstborn,
> The troops everywhere in the country he ordered under his (command).
> He let (everything) go, entrusted the kingship to him
> And, himself, he started out for a long journey.[56]

Despite the uniqueness of a crown prince's being officially recognized as regent, from these sources it is nevertheless evident that Belshazzar was regent.

There are no cuneiform documents for the last years of Nabonidus' reign which mention Belshazzar. The defective *Nabonidus Chronicle* carries him only to the eleventh regnal year, and known contract tablets only to the fourteenth year.[57] Belshazzar is not mentioned by name in any of the three Persian accounts of the fall of Babylon. The *Cyrus Cylinder* furnishes propaganda for Cyrus' rule, but does not give a circumstantial account of the capture of the city. The *Nabonidus Chronicle* speaks of "the son of the king" without giving a name, and the *Persian Verse Account* merely speaks of "his eldest, firstborn

---

50 *Ibid.*, p. 94.
51 *Ibid.*, p. 96.
52. *ANET*, pp. 309-310, n. 5.
53 Dougherty, *op. cit.*, pp. 101-102.
54 *ANET*, pp. 305 f.
55 S. S. Smith, *Babylonian Historical Texts Relating to the Capture and Downfall of Babylon* (London: Methuen & Co., Ltd., 1924), pp. 100, 119; Dougherty, *op. cit.*, p. 107.
56 *ANET*, pp. 313 f.
57 Dougherty, *op. cit.*, p. 191.

son" both of which titles in other texts are used in connection with the name of Belshazzar.[58]

Two chief perplexities remain in the Biblical account of Belshazzar. The first is that in Daniel Nebuchadnezzar is called his father (Dan. 5:2, 11, 18). Also Josephus speaks of Baltasaros' fall as the end of the descendants (*eggonas*) of Nebuchadnezzar.[59] Nabonidus, father of Belshazzar in the cuneiform sources, however, was neither a son nor a descendant of Nebuchadnezzar. Instead, he, likely from a prominent family, is a usurper of the throne.[60] Dougherty argues that there may be some reason to conjecture that Nabonidus married Nitocris, daughter of Nebuchadnezzar, and that she is the mother of Belshazzar.[61] In this argument Belshazzar becomes the grandson of Nebuchadnezzar. "Son" and "father" are used elsewhere in Scripture for remote kinship (cf. I Kings 15:11; II Kings 14:3; 18:3; Isa. 51:2; Gen. 28:13; II Sam. 9:7). However, the case still remains in the realm of conjecture.

The other problem is that of his title: "the Chaldean king" (Dan. 5:30; cf. 5:1; 8:1); and around the point of whether or not he actually had the title of king, the current discussion of Belshazzar centers. Dougherty pointed out that every fully dated cuneiform document of the period in question mentions Nabonidus as king and that complete royal authority is not ascribed to Belshazzar by any record upon clay. It is also noticed that the New Year's festival could not be held because Nabonidus was absent from Babylon. Nabonidus is the king, and Belshazzar is the son of the king. H. H. Rowley argues that there is grave historical error on the point in the book of Daniel and insists that arguments based upon the *Persian Verse Account* which transmits a text from Nabonidus' third year, alluded to above ("He let everything go, he entrusted the kingship to him"[62]), are overworked arguments.[63] On the contrary side, Edward J. Young argues that though Belshazzar may not have had the title of king, it was proper for Daniel to date events by his regnal years since he exercised the function of king.[64] He

---

58 *Ibid.*, p. 181.
59 *Ant.* x. 11. 4 (247-248).
60 Dougherty, *op. cit.*, p. 18.
61 *Ibid.*, pp. 51 ff.
62 *ANET*, p. 313.
63 "The Historicity of the Fifth Chapter of Daniel," *JTS*, XXXII (1930-1931), 12-31.
64 *The Prophecy of Daniel, A Commentary* (Grand Rapids: Eerdmans, 1949), pp. 115-119.

readily grants, however, that official documents were dated by the reign of Nabonidus.

Summary

Brief as the Neo-Babylonian kingdom was — not extending longer than seventy years — it has furnished us the names of five rulers: Merodach-baladan, Nebuchadnezzar, Evil-Merodach, Nergalsharezer, and Belshazzar. The first of these, as we have pointed out in the beginning of this section, precedes the establishment of the kingdom, but is of none the less interest for that fact.

V

THE MEN OF ISRAEL AND JUDAH

The archives, the tombs, and the monumental steles of the Israelite and Judean kings have up to this time not been discovered. We know chronicles were kept from appeals made to them by the writers of the books of Kings and of Chronicles, but we do not have them. The only royal inscription of a Palestinian king of the Israelite period that has been found in Palestine to date is that of Mesha, king of Moab, at which we have looked earlier in this study.

The records of the near neighbors of Israel — the Philistines, the Edomites, the Ammonites, the Syrians, and the Tyreans — in which we might expect to find allusions dealing with Israelite figures have for the most part also not been discovered. There have been found in Palestine a few Egyptian steles and perhaps slightly more than twenty cuneiform tablets, both of which groups date chiefly from the second millennium B.C. before Israel became dominant in Palestine. But, apart from groups of potsherds found in Samaria, Lachish, and Arad and isolated sherds found in various sites, and apart from a few seals, we have no written records from Palestine contemporary with the Old Testament period except the Bible itself. We are therefore largely dependent upon Assyrian records as we try to find the names of Biblical characters.

Some of the seals found in Palestine and some of the sherds have Hebrew names on them that are parallel to some Biblical names; however, in most cases there is no solid basis upon which to conjecture that their possessors are identical with Biblical figures. The few exceptions we will notice as we proceed.

Existing archaeological sources and the Biblical sources are interested in the figures of Israel and Judah for two entirely different reasons. The Bible concentrates on their religious activities, but about these matters the archaeological sources say nothing. The archaeological materials, on the other hand, deal with their political, economic, and military affairs; but such affairs are in some cases passed over in complete silence in the Bible and in others are mentioned only incidentally. Consequently most of the material we survey is of value for supplementing and for illustrating Biblical sources. For only a few events is there really a direct contact in the two types of sources.

In this segment of our study — as has been true in the others — we are impressed with the lateness with which our figures appear on the scene of history. Adam, Noah, Abraham, Jacob, Moses, Joshua, Samuel, Saul, David, and Solomon — all must be passed by in silence. It has often been noticed that the names of figures like Abraham, Jacob, Haran, and Nahor do have parallels in records of the Middle East, but there is not the slightest basis upon which to attempt an identification with the well-known Biblical figures. Certain structures are conjecturally thought to be those of Saul and of Solomon, but this is not due to the fact that written records attach names to these structures. It is not until we come to Omri that we are on more solid footing.

MEN OF ISRAEL

Omri

Omri, who came to the throne of the northern kingdom by choice of the army following the assassination of Elah, founded the Omride dynasty, which continued through three generations until its violent end at the hands of Jehu. Omri reigned from about 876 to 869 B.C., but little space is devoted to him by the writer of the book of Kings (I Kings 16:16-28). He promptly overcame his usurper opponent Zimri, murderer of Elah, whose reign had been limited to seven days (I Kings 16:15-18). A further struggle with Tibni also eventually ended victoriously (I Kings 16:21). Though given credit for reigning six years in Tirzah, for purchasing the hill of Samaria, for fortifying the hill, and for moving the capital of Israel there from Tirzah (thereby laying the basis for using the name "Samaria" for the entire northern kingdom), an adverse verdict is passed upon him for his religious policy: "Omri did what was evil in the sight of the Lord, and did more evil than all who were before him" (I Kings 16:25). The prophet Micah spoke reproachfully of the "statutes of Omri" (Micah 6:16).

There are only small hints in Scripture of the international significance of Omri:

> Now the rest of the acts of Omri which he did, and the might that he showed, are they not written in the Book of the Chronicles of the Kings of Israel? (I Kings 16:27).

But as previously noted, we do not have access to the sources alluded to. The marriage of his eldest son, Ahab, to Jezebel, the daughter of Ethbaal (Ittobaal) the Sidonian king (I Kings 16:31), was likely the cementing of an alliance which had immediate benefits as a check against the rival power Aram, but brought eventual disaster to the dynasty.

It is from the Mesha stele that we learn that Omri conquered Moab and controlled Transjordan north of the Arnon River, an event not mentioned in the Bible. Mesha boasts,

> (Now) Omri had occupied the land of Medeba and (Israel) had dwelt there in his time and half the time of his son (Ahab), forty years; but Chemosh dwelt there in my time.[1]

Not only did Omri come to the notice of Mesha, but something of his international significance is to be seen in the fact that Assyria, throughout its history even a century after Omri's death, referred to Israel as *Bit Humri* or *Bit Humria* (House of Omri) and referred to her kings as *Mar Huumrii* (Son of Omri). This practice is ironically true even in the case of Jehu who had in reality assassinated the whole house of Omri.[2] Evidence for Omri comes from the reign of the four kings: Shalmaneser III, Adad-nirari III, Tiglath-pileser III, and Sargon II.

From the reign of Shalmaneser III, there are two items. First is a fragment of an annalistic text which reads:

> At that time I received the tribute of the inhabitants of Tyre, Sidon, and of Jehu, son of Omri.[3]

Second there is the Black Obelisk which records "tribute of Jehu, son of Omri. . . ."[4]

From the reign of Adad-nirari III, a stone slab found at Calah lists those who have submitted to him. Among them we find:

---

1 *ANET,* p. 320. "Ahab" which is not in the text has been supplied by the translator. For the problem involved see above p. 63.

2 *Ibid.,* pp. 280, 281.

3 *Ibid.,* p. 280.

4 *Ibid.,* p. 281.

. . . from the banks of the Euphrates, the country of the Hittites, Amurru-country in its full extent, Tyre, Sidon, Israel (*mat Hu-um-ri*), Edom, Palestine (*Pa-la-as-tu*), as far as the shore of the Great Sea of the Setting Sun, I made them all submit to my feet, imposing upon them tribute.[5]

Tiglath-pileser III furnishes three items. First there is an annalistic record:

. . . Abilakka which are adjacent to Israel (*Bit Hu-um-ri-a*) [and the] wide (land of) [Naphta]li, in its entire extent, I united with Assyria.[6]

Then there is a second passage from the same annal:

Israel (lit.: "Omri-Land" *Bit Humria*) . . . all its inhabitants (and) their possessions I led to Assyria.[7]

Third is a fragmentary inscription from Nimrud:

Similarly Israel, to whose northern border reference is made, is called "the territory of the house of Omri" ((*mat*) *bit-*(*m*)*humri*) as it had been in the earlier annals of Shalmaneser (cf. Adad-nirari III; I R. 35, I, 12; (*mat*) *hu-um-ri-i*).[8]

Sargon II left two cases. First, a pavement at the gate of his palace:

(Property of Sargon, etc. King of Assyria, etc.) conqueror of Samaria (*Sa-mir-i-na*) and of the entire (country of) Israel (*Bit Hu-um-ri-a*).[9]

Second, annals of Room XIV list victories:

I conquered and sacked the towns Shinuhtu (and) Samaria, and all Israel (*Bit Hu-um-ri-ia*).[10]

Ahab

Considerably more space (I Kings 16:29–22:40) is devoted by Scripture to Ahab than to his predecessor Omri despite the

---

5 *Ibid.*
6 *Ibid.*, p. 283.
7 *Ibid.*, p. 284.
8 D. J. Wiseman, "A Fragmentary Inscription of Tiglath-Pileser III from Nimrud," *Iraq*, XVIII (1956), 121, 123.
9 *ANET*, p. 284.
10 *Ibid.*, p. 285.

fact that Ahab is overshadowed by Elijah. The verdict of the Biblical historian upon the total reign of Ahab is entirely adverse: "And Ahab the son of Omri did evil in the sight of the Lord more than all that were before him" (I Kings 16:30). His marriage to Jezebel and the subsequent effort to foster the worship of Baal in Israel, including the building of a temple in Samaria (I Kings 16:32), brought stiff opposition from the prophet Elijah. That prophet, at considerable risk to himself, stemmed the tide of syncretism.

Ahab's kingdom was unsuccessfully invaded by Arameans of Damascus (I Kings 20:1-21). In Transjordan he was victorious in the battle at Aphek (I Kings 20:26), but he finally lost his life in a battle at Ramoth-gilead and was brought back to Samaria and buried (I Kings 22:29-38).

It was none of these affairs that attracted the attention of those outside of Israel who have left records. Ahab is remembered for an event entirely passed over in silence in the Bible. Faced with the westward expansion of the Assyrians led by Shalmaneser III, Ahab and his allies — a federation of twelve kings in the west — met the Assyrian at Qarqar on the Orontes River in 853 B.C. This first known direct contact between Israel and Assyria seems to have ended indecisively, but Shalmaneser claims a great victory. On the stele which was discovered in 1861 at Kurkh (ancient Tushkha) on the Tigris in Turkey and which is now preserved in the British Museum (No. 118884), Shalmaneser's record of the affair is found. Second in the list of the allies is "Ahab the Israelite" with 2,000 chariots and 10,000 foot soldiers. Ahab commands the largest complement of chariots in the list but is second to the king of Damascus in foot soldiers.

Shalmaneser summarizes his victory:

> I slew 14,000 of their soldiers with the sword, descending upon them like Adad when he makes a rainstorm pour down. I spread their corpses (everywhere), filling the entire plain with their widely scattered (fleeing) soldiers. During the battle, I made their blood flow down the *hur-pa-lu* of the district. The plain was too small to let (all) their (text: his) souls descend (into the nether world), the vast field gave out (when it came) to bury them. With their (text: sing.) corpses I spanned the Orontes before there was a bridge. Even during the battle I took from them their chariots, their horses broken to the yoke.[11]

---

11 *Ibid.*, p. 279.

Jehu

Jehu's usurpation, following the death of Ahab at Ramoth-gilead *ca.* 850 B.C. and the death of Ahab's two successors, Ahaziah (II Kings 1:2, 17) and Jehoram (II Kings 3:6; 9:23-24), brought to a violent end the dynasty of the Omrides. Jehu's bloody revolt in the area of Jezreel was stimulated by the prophet Elisha (I Kings 19:15-18), but was actually touched off by an unnamed prophet (II Kings 9:1-3). Jezebel's innovations had met a vigorous counter attack (II Kings 10:1-27).

The new dynasty established by Jehu continued about a century before it met its tragic end with the murder of Zechariah by Shallum. Despite its having happened a century before, the prophet Hosea in the middle of the eighth century shortly before Shallum's revolt, was still calling attention to the violence of Jehu's revolt (Hosea 1:4).

It was not the internal religious or political problems and policies of Jehu's reign of twenty-eight years (I Kings 10:11; cf. II Chron. 22:8-9) that made its way into the records preserved on the monuments. Unlike his predecessor, Ahab, who with his allies had been partially successful in resisting Shalmaneser III, Jehu at an unknown date (perhaps *ca.* 841)[12] came to terms with and became a vassal of Assyria. The episode and its details are not mentioned in the Bible, but are known from a stele set up by Shalmaneser.

A. H. Layard in 1846 found the Black Obelisk of Shalmaneser which is now to be seen in the British Museum (No. 118885).[13] In the second panel from the top, Jehu is depicted on his knees in a low turban and a long over-garment. This is the earliest picture of an Israelite to survive and is the only known contemporary, ancient, artistic representation of an Israelite king. In the cuneiform above the picture is written:

> The tribute of Jehu, son of Omri, I received from him silver, gold, a golden *saplu* bowl, a golden vase with pointed bottom, golden tumblers, golden buckets, tin, a staff for a king (and) wooden *puruhtu*.[14]

We have earlier seen that Shalmaneser on a fragmentary annalistic text also declares:

---

12 R. D. Barnett, *Illustrations of Old Testament History* (London: The British Museum, 1966), p. 46.

13 *Nineveh and Its Remains* (London: John Murray, 1849), I, 346-348.

14 *ANET*, p. 281; cf. Ernst Michel, "Die Assur-Texte Salmanassars III (858-824)," *Die Welt des Orients*, II (1955), 137-139.

At that time I received the tribute of the inhabitants of Tyre, Sidon, and of Jehu, son of Omri.[15]

It is ironical to notice that in both of these texts Jehu is called "son of Omri," despite the fact that in reality he is not at all related and is the overthrower of that house.

Jehoash

Joash (Jehoash), son of Jehoahaz, reigned over Israel for sixteen years (801-786 B.C.) and is said to have fought successfully against Amaziah, king of Judah, and to have broken down the wall of Jerusalem (II Kings 14:8-14). During the last illness of Elisha, Joash went to visit him, and the prophet by a series of symbolic acts promised him victory over his enemies, the Syrians (II Kings 13:14-19). Joash proceeded to take from Ben-hadad the lands that Joash's father had lost to Hazael. The victories of Joash laid the basis for the glorious reign of his son Jeroboam II, during which time Israel reached her greatest heights. The standard adverse verdict on northern kings for following the ways of Jeroboam, the son of Nebat, is pronounced by the writer of the book of Kings against Joash. He had reigned in Samaria and was buried there (II Kings 13:10-13).

The general background of this period can be filled out from the records of Adad-nirari III (810-782 B.C.) who claims to have subjected the "Amurru-country to its full extent, Tyre, Sidon, Israel (mat-Hu-um-ri), Edom, Palestine (Pa-la-as-tu) as far as the shore of the Great Sea of the setting Sun."[16] He further claims at this time to have marched against Damascus. Furthermore, the Aramaic Zakir inscription, thought to date ca. 805 B.C., tells of an unsuccessful expedition of "Bar-hadad bar Hazael, king of Aram" against Zakir, "king of Hamath and La^cath."[17] This inscription corroborates the succession of kings faced by Joash.

As recently as autumn of 1968, results of an expedition in 1967 of the British School of Archaeology in Iraq to a site, Tell al Rimah, near Mosul were published. A stela standing about four feet in height of Adad-nirari III contains the form of the king with about twenty lines of text on the skirt. There are references to the city of Samaria and to King Jehoash. The king claims in his first year (806 B.C.) to have made the land of Amurru and the Hatti land in its entirety kneel at his feet.

---

15 *ANET*, p. 280.
16 *Ibid.*, p. 281.
17 *Ibid.*, p. 655.

"He received the tribute of Ia'asu the Samaritan, of the Tyrian (ruler) and of the Sidonian (ruler)." It has been argued that *Ia'asu* of the inscription is Jehoash and that the date discrepancy involved is to be explained on the basis that two campaigns of the king have been conflated. The Bible does not refer to Adad-nirari by name and does not refer to tribute given by Joash to an Assyrian monarch. This inscription is the earliest known non-Biblical reference to the city of Samaria by this name.[18]

Jeroboam II

The reign of Jeroboam II is the Indian summer of the northern kingdom. During his forty-one years (786-746 B.C.) — the longest reign for any northern king — Israel's territory was extended from the entrance of Hamath as far as the sea of the Arabah (II Kings 14:25). There is a brief allusion to his wars, but the same adverse verdict that is passed over all the northern kings also is passed over Jeroboam by the historian, and only seven verses are devoted to him (II Kings 14:23-29).

Amos (1:1) and Hosea (1:1) are dated in his reign and Jonah, son of Amittai, is said to have predicted his successes (II Kings 14:25). Amos is accused by Amaziah, priest of Bethel, with conspiring against Jeroboam and with threatening his death (Amos 7:10-11).

Jeroboam has found no place in the annals of his neighbors. His free expansion in territory is doubtless due to the fact that his reign corresponded to a period of decline in Assyria which according to the Eponym List permitted only five campaigns against Damascus and Hamath in this period. But these campaigns kept these neighbors of Israel occupied and left Jeroboam to follow his own inclinations.

The seal found by Schumacher at Megiddo in 1904 which was decorated with a roaring lion, but which has since been lost, has the Hebrew inscription "Belonging to Shema, the minister (*ᶜebed*) of Jeroboam." The *ᶜebed* type seal, of which there are several examples, belonged to royal officials. One cannot be certain which of the Jeroboams is meant — Jeroboam I (I Kings 12:12 ff.) or Jeroboam II (II Kings 14:23 ff.). Ordinarily it is attributed to Jeroboam II,[19] but S. Yeivin just a few years ago

18 Stephanie Page, "A Stela of Adad-Nirari III and Nergal-Eres from Tell al Rimah," *Iraq*, XXX (1968), 139-153; D. J. Wiseman, "Old Testament Evidence," *Christianity Today*, XIII (Jan. 3, 1969), 319.

19 D. W. Thomas, *Documents from Old Testament Times* (New York: Harper and Brothers, 1961), pp. 220, 221.

argued for Jeroboam I on the basis of paleography, art styles, and the level in the tell at which the seal was found.[20]

Menahem

Menahem, son of Gadi (*ca.* 745-738 B.C.), as did the majority of Israelite rulers in the chaotic times of the late Israelite kingdom, came to the throne by violence. Coming from Tirzah to Samaria, he slew Shallum who had reigned for only one month and then seized the throne (II Kings 15:14). He proceeded to seize Tappuah and its territory from Tirzah on and slew the pregnant women in it.

The insecurity of his position is revealed in the fact that when Pul (Tiglath-pileser III) came against Menahem, he gave him a thousand talents of silver to help him maintain his hold on the throne. Menahem obtained the money by levying a tax of fifty shekels of silver each upon every wealthy man (II Kings 15:19-20). After a reign of ten years, Menahem died in peace (II Kings 15:17, 22) and was the only one of the last six kings of Israel to do so.

Tiglath-pileser in an annalistic text relates his relationship with Menahem:

> I received tribute from Kushtashpi of Compagene (kummuhu), Rezon (*Ra-hi-a-nu*) of Damascus (Saimerisu), Menahem of Samaria (*Me-ni-hi-im meal Sa-me-ri-na-a-a*), Hiram (*Hiru-um-mu*) of Tyre. . . .[21]

Yet another fragmentary text in which the name has been reconstructed reads:

> [as for Menahem I ov]erpowered him [like a snowstorm] and he . . . fled like a bird, alone [and bowed to my feet (?)] I returned him to his place [and imposed tribute upon him to wit:] gold, silver, linen garments with multicolored trimmings, . . . great . . . [I re]ceived from him. Israel (lit.: "Omri-Land" *Bit Humria*) . . . all its inhabitants (and) their possessions I led to Assyria.[22]

---

20 "The Date of the Seal 'Belonging to Shema^c (the) Servant (of) Jeroboam,'" *JNES*, XIX (1960), 205-212.

21 *ANET*, p. 283.

22 *Ibid.*, p. 284; cf. M. Noth, *Die israelitischen Personennamen* (Stuttgart: W. Kohlhammer, 1928; Reprografischer Nachdruck: Hildesheim: Georg Olms, 1966), p. 222; D. J. Wiseman, "The Nimrud Tablets," *Iraq*, XV (1953), 135.

Pekah

Pekah, son of Remaliah, came to the throne of Israel by violence as his immediate predecessors and successor did. With
the aid of fifty Gileadites he slew Pekahiah in Samaria and
seized the throne (II Kings 15:25). The writer of the book of
Kings gives the standard adverse verdict on his reign of twenty
years (II Kings 15:28).

In a reversal of alliances and enemies such as have been
seen many times in history, Pekah and Rezin joined together to
overthrow Ahaz and to replace him with the son of Tabeel, but
were unable to do so (Isa. 7:1, 6-7; II Chron. 28:5 ff.). Ahaz's
counter move brought Tiglath-pileser III into the picture and
Pekah lost large sections of his territory.

> In the days of Pekah, king of Israel, Tiglath-pileser, king of
> Assyria came and captured Ijon, Abel-beth-maacah, Janoah,
> Kedesh, Hazor, Gilead, and Galilee, all the land of Naphtali,
> and he carried the people captive to Assyria (II Kings 15:29).

Pekah's reign came to an end, as it had begun, in violence.
Hoshea, the son of Elah, conspired against him, slew him, and
reigned in his stead (II Kings 15:30).

It is this last episode of his career which is recorded by Tiglath-pileser III in an annalistic text:

> They overthrew their king Pekah (*Pa-qa-ha*) and I placed
> Hoshea (*A-u-si'*) as king over them. . . .[23]

Y. Yadin found a jar in Hazor in stratum V, the level destroyed by Tiglath-pileser III in 734 B.C., which is inscribed with
the name "Pekah."[24] The name is striking, but in the absence
of other evidence, it cannot be definitely connected with the
king.

Hoshea

The northern kingdom, following a period of great instability
in which regicide was common, found its last king in Hoshea,
who had conspired against and had murdered Pekah (II Kings
15:30). Hoshea was at first tributary to Tiglath-pileser III, but
following the Assyrian's death (*ca.* 727 B.C.), Hoshea revolted
and brought the wrath of Shalmaneser V upon himself: Shal-

---

23 *ANET*, p. 284.
24 *Hazor* (Jerusalem: Magnes Press, The Hebrew University, 1960), II,
73 f.

maneser, king of Assyria, came up against Hoshea who "became his servant and paid him tribute" (II Kings 17:3).

After a period of paying his tribute, Hoshea plotted with So, king of Egypt, and was arrested (II Kings 17:4).[25] Assyria besieged the city of Samaria for three years, but it fell in 721 and its people were exiled (cf. II Kings 18:9-10).

Tiglath-pileser III records this last exchange of northern kings which brought Hoshea to the throne in a fragmentary annalistic text:

> They overthrew their king Pekah (Pa-qa-ha) and I placed Hoshea (A-ú-si') as king over them. I received from them 10 talents of gold, 1,000 (?) talents of silver as their [tri]bute and brought them to Assyria.[26]

The Assyrian accounts of the fall of Samaria and of the exiling of its people do not mention the name of the Israelite king in this connection.

MEN OF JUDAH

Uzziah

Uzziah (ca. 783-742 B.C.), whose alternate name in Scripture is Azariah (Azariah: II Kings 15:1, 6-8, 23, 27; Uzziah: II Kings 15:13, 30, 32, 34; Isa. 1:1; 6:1; 7:1; Hos. 1:1; Amos. 1:1; Zech. 14:5) reigned over Judah longer than any other king. However, the book of Kings devotes only seven verses to his reign of fifty-two years. The book of Chronicles (II Chron. 26:1 ff.) records his restoration of Elath to Judah, his wars against the Philistines, and his subjecting the Ammonites to tribute. He built towers in Jerusalem, maintained an army in readiness, and was known afar. Nevertheless, Uzziah was smitten with leprosy in his last years and dwelt in a separate house while his son governed the people.

It has been heatedly debated whether or not the records of Tiglath-pileser III mention Azariah (Uzziah). Two fragmentary texts engraved on slabs found at Calah are relevant to the question. In the first the name of the country is clear, but the personal name of the king is a partial reconstruction. In the second[27] the personal name is clear, but no country is given.

---

25 "So King of Egypt," see above, pp. 20-22
26 ANET, p. 284.
27 H. M. Haydn, "Azariah of Judah and Tiglath-pileser III," JBL, XXVIII (1909), 182-183.

The first reads in part:

> [In] the (subsequent) course of my campaign [I recived]
> the tribute of kin[gs . . . A]zriau from Iuda (*Ia-u-da-a-a*),
> like a [. . . Azr]iau from Iuda in . . . countless, (reaching)
> sky high . . . eyes, like from heaven . . . etc.[28]

E. Schrader argued that the chronicle is dealing with events perhaps connected with the years 742-740 B.C., but Tadmor now assigns them to 738 B.C. Schrader held that the text dealt with the Judean king,[29] but H. Winckler maintained that the text may refer to a king of one of the Syrian neighbors of Israel.[30] Sidney Smith, a generation ago, declared it an open question,[31] but current opinion is swinging back to an acceptance of the identification with Uzziah,[32] and if correct, Uzziah becomes the first southern figure mentioned in Assyrian records.

Two seals are known which belonged to officials of king Uzziah.

(a) "(belonging) to Shebanio (the) servant (of king) 'Uzzio."[33]

(b) "(belonging) to 'Abio (the) servant (of king) 'Uzzio."[34]

The tombs of the Judean kings have not been discovered though Josephus reports the opening of the tomb of David by Hyrcanus in the Maccabean period.[35] A tomb inscription — not contemporary with Uzziah, but at least six hundred years after his death — has been discovered in the Russian Museum on the Mount of Olives. The catalogue and other important information

28 *ANET*, p. 282.
29 *The Cuneiform Inscriptions and the Old Testament* (London: Williams and Norgate, 1885), I, 208 ff.; cf. Haydn, *op. cit.*, pp. 182-199.
30 "Das syrische Land Yaudi und der angebliche Azarja von Juda," *Altorientalische Forchungen*, I (1893), 1-23.
31 "The Supremacy of Assyria," *CAH*, III, 35 ff.
32 W. W. Hallo, "From Qarqar to Carchemish: Assyria and Israel in the Light of New Discoveries," *BA*, XXIII (1960), 47; H. Tadmor, "Azriyau of Yaudi," *Scripta Hierosolymitana*, VIII (1961), 232-271.
33 D. Diringer, *Le inscrizioni antico-ebraiche palestinesi* (Firenze: Felice Le Monnier, 1934), pp. 223-224, Pl. XXI, 1; M. A. Levy, *Siegel und Gemmen* (Breslau: Schlettr'schen Buchhandlung, 1869), pp. 39-41, Pl. III, 6.
34 Diringer, *op. cit.*, pp. 221-222, Pl. XXI, 2; Levy, *op cit.*, pp. 41-42, Pl. III, 9; also cited in S. Yeivin, "The Date of the Seal 'Belonging to Shema^c (the) Servant (of) Jeroboam,'" *JNES*, XIX (1960), 207, n. 11.
35 *Ant.* xiii. 8. 4 (249); *War* i. 2. 5 (61).

of the museum were destroyed in World War I. Consequently, no information is available on where this stone was found and how it came to the museum. It was discovered there by E. L. Sukenik. More recently it has been removed to the Patriarchate in New York. The stone block is thirty-five centimeters square. The excellently preserved Aramaic script is characteristic of the period 130 B.C.-A.D. 70. The block reads:

Hither were brought the bones of King Uzziah — Do not open!

The stone attests veneration of the graves of important figures and demonstrates that the people of the period of the inscription thought that they were moving the bones of the king.[36]

Jotham

Jotham, son of Uzziah and successor of Uzziah, after the latter contracted leprosy, reigned jointly with his father for eight years (*ca.* 750-742 B.C.), but later reigned in his own right for an equal number of years (*ca.* 742-735 B.C.). The total number of years given in Scripture for his reign is sixteen and this figure likely includes both of these periods (II Kings 15:33; II Chron. 27:1). Jotham built the upper gate of the house of the Lord and cities, forts, and towers in the hill country of Judah (II Kings 15:35; II Chron. 27:3-4). He successfully fought against the Ammonites (II Chron. 27:5), but already his kingdom was threatened by the alliance to force him into conflict with Assyria (II Kings 15:36). The stereotyped adverse verdict of the book of Kings is passed upon Jotham for his failure to remove the high places.

Nelson Glueck found a signet ring enclosed in a copper casing at Ezion Geber which is now in the Smithsonian Museum.[37] The ring has the picture of a horned ram with what Glueck conjectures to be the form of a man in front of him. N. Avigad, on the other hand, has more recently argued that the object in front of the ram is a bellows or an ingot of copper.[38] Inscribed in retrograde in Hebrew characters are the letters *"lytm"* i.e., "belonging to Jotham." It is likely, though it cannot be proved with certainty, that it is the king of Judah to whom the ring belonged. Uzziah had built and restored Elath to Judah (II Kings

---

36 W. F. Albright, "The Discovery of an Aramaic Inscription Relating to King Uzziah," *BASOR*, No. 44 (1931), 8-10.

37 "The Third Season of Excavation at Tell El-Kheleifeh," *BASOR*, No. 79 (1940), 13 ff.

38 "The Jotham Seal from Elath," *BASOR*, No. 163 (Oct. 1961), 18-22.

14:22; II Chron. 26:1-2) and it remained in Judean control briefly until the time of Ahaz. About 735 B.C. the Edomites drove the Judeans out.

Ahaz

Young Ahaz, king of Judah 735-715 B.C., confronted with a combined attack of Pekah and Rezin in what is known as the Syro-Ephraimitic war (*ca.* 734 B.C.), was terrified. Picturesquely Isaiah says: "his heart and the heart of his people shook as the trees of the forest shake before the wind" (Isa. 7:2). His opponents planned to depose him and to replace him with the "son of Tabeel" (Isa. 7:6). It is likely that it was in the face of this danger that Ahaz offered his son as a burnt offering (II Kings 16:3; II Chron. 28:3). Though the kings were not able to conquer Jerusalem, many Judeans were killed and numerous captives were taken, but later these were released at Jericho at the insistence of the prophet Oded (II Chron. 28:8 ff.). The Edomites took advantage of the crisis to recover Elath from Judah (I Kings 16:6), and at this time the Philistines also made inroads on Judean territory (II Chron. 28:17).

While Ahaz made plans to secure the aid of Tiglath-pileser III, Isaiah roundly denounced the plan (Isa. 7), but failed to convince the king. Ahaz proceeded to appeal to Assyria.

> I am your servant. . . . Come up and rescue me from the hand of the king of Syria and from the hand of the king of Israel who are attacking me (II Kings 16:7).

Ahaz accompanied his plea with a present from the temple treasure and from the royal treasure. Tiglath-pileser acted, captured Damascus in 732 B.C., exiled its people to Kir, and at the same time killed Rezin its king (II Kings 16:7-9). At this same time Tiglath-pileser also conquered and exiled portions of Israel.

Ahaz went to Damascus to make his submission to Assyria. While there, he was enamored with an altar he saw and proceeded to have it duplicated and set up in the temple in Jerusalem. The old altar was set aside, and the king used the new one in sacrifice. He also removed the bronze calves from under the sea in the temple court and put a pediment of stone in their place (II Kings 16:17).

Prior to Ahaz's submission to Assyria, Isaiah warned that Ahaz's plans would bring him into dire straits as serious as anything that had happened since the division of the kingdom (Isa. 7:

17). The book of Chronicles remarks concerning his dealings with Assyria: "So Tiglath-pilneser king of Assyria came against him and afflicted him instead of strengthening him" (II Chron. 28:20).

The burial of Ahaz was in Jerusalem, but not in the royal tombs (II Chron. 28:27).

The archaeological items relevant to Ahaz are two. Among a list of tribute payers of Syro-Palestine, Tiglath-pileser III lists Ahaz, to whom he gives the fuller name Jehoahaz:

> . . . Mitinti of Ashkelon, Jehoahaz (*Ia-u-ha-zi*) of Judah (*Ia-u-du-a-a*), Kaushmalaku of Edom (*U-du-mu-a-a*), Muzr[i . . .], Hanno (*Ha-a-nu-ú-nu*) of Gaza (*Ha-za-at-a-a*) (consisting of) gold, silver, tin, iron, antimony, linen garments with multi-colored trimmings, garments of their native industries (being made of) dark purple wool . . . all kinds of costly objects be they products of the sea or of the continent, the (choice) products of their regions, the treasures of (their) kings, horses, mules (trained for) the yoke. . . .[39]

In addition to this notice in the Assyrian records, there is also a carnelian seal from an unknown provenience but which is inscribed with the Hebrew words in the style of writing of Ahaz's period:

> "Seal of Asna (?), Official of Ahaz."

The seal was purchased from a dealer by Edward T. Newell. *ᶜEbed* seals of this type were ordinarily the property of high ranking officials, but we cannot conjecture exactly what position in Ahaz's administration this official filled.[40]

Hezekiah

Hezekiah, in whose reign the prophets Isaiah (Isa. 1:1) and Micah (Micah 1:1) are said to have prophesied, attracts attention in the Bible for being one of the reforming kings of Judah. Contrary to that for most of the kings, an unqualified, favorable verdict is passed on his reign. Coming to the throne at the age of twenty-five, Hezekiah is assigned twenty-nine years by the historian (II Kings 18:2; II Chron. 29:1). He is praised for removing the high places (II Kings 18:4), for trusting in the

---

39 *ANET*, p. 282; cf. Thomas, *op. cit.*, pp. 56-57.

40 C. C. Torrey, "A Hebrew Seal from the Reign of Ahaz," *BASOR*, No. 79 (1940), 27-28; "A Few Ancient Seals," *AASOR*, II & III (1921-1922), 106-108.

Lord as none before him nor after him did, for rebelling against the king of Assyria, and for smiting the Philistines as far as Gaza (II Kings 18:3-8). The book of Chronicles attributes to him major temple repairs and sanctification ceremonies (II Chron. 29: 1 ff.). Though these reforms are not extensively described in Kings, the Rabshakeh in his speech refers to Hezekiah's destroying the high places (II Kings 18:22). Hezekiah held a Passover celebration to which both northern and southern peoples were invited (II Chron. 30:1 ff.). One of the collections in the book of Proverbs is said to have been copied out by his men (Prov. 25:29).

There are major chronological problems connected with Hezekiah's reign, in particular arising out of I Kings 18:9-10 where the siege of Samaria begins in Hezekiah's fourth year and the city falls in his sixth year. Certain Old Testament chronological systems reject this evidence and date Hezekiah's reign from 715 B.C. to 687 B.C. in order to harmonize I Kings 18:13 (which assigns Sennacherib's invasion to the fourteenth year of Hezekiah) with chronological data for the same event obtained from Assyrian sources. Other systems attempt to solve the problem by the expediency of co-regencies and date the beginning of Hezekiah's reign to 729 B.C.

Sargon made a campaign against Ashdod in 711 B.C. in which he claims Ashdod sought aid from Judah and Egypt.[41] Hezekiah is not here mentioned by name; no reprisals were taken on him; hence we conclude he did not join the revolt. In fact, there is no reason to suppose that Hezekiah revolted at all until after Sargon's death in 705 B.C.

Anticipating the possibility of a siege, Hezekiah made changes in the water system of Jerusalem in order to bring the waters of the Gihon spring into the city of Jerusalem (II Kings 20:20; II Chron. 32:30). It is usually assumed that the 1749 foot tunnel which today connects the Virgin's fountain with the pool of Siloam is Hezekiah's work. Its inscription has been removed to the Istanbul Museum.[42]

With the accession of Sennacherib to the throne, Hezekiah ceased paying his tribute (II Kings 18:7). Sennacherib came against the fortified cities of Judah and seized them (II Kings 18:13). One of these fortress cities was Lachish, and from there Sennacherib sent his Rabshakeh to demand Hezekiah's surren-

41 *ANET,* p. 287.
42 *Ibid.,* p. 321; G. E. Wright, *Biblical Archaeology* (Philadelphia: Westminster Press, 1962), pp. 172-174.

der. Bas-reliefs found in Sennacherib's palace depict him on his throne as the spoil of Lachish is carried before him.

15. SENNACHERIB RECEIVING TRIBUTE from subject peoples. Courtesy, British Museum

We have earlier, when dealing with Sennacherib, discussed Sennacherib's invasion which is related by both II Kings and by Isaiah (II Kings 18 ff.; Isa. 36 ff.) in sections that are almost word for word identical. The invasion is also surveyed in II Chronicles 32. We will not here discuss again these sections except to point out that Sennacherib's account supplements the Biblical account by giving the details of Hezekiah's revolt. The Philistine states deposed the Assyrian puppet Padi, king of Ekron, who refused to join their revolt and delivered him to Hezekiah for safe keeping. Eventually Hezekiah was forced to deliver him up. Sennacherib claims to have re-established Padi on his throne and to have taken reprisals on the rebels.

The details of the revolt and the invasion, as we have earlier noticed, are related in Sennacherib's annals known in five copies, which include the Chicago prism, the Taylor prism, and the more recently found Nimrud prism. Three times these records mention Hezekiah's name. About Hezekiah's role Sennacherib says:

> The officials, the patricians and the (common) people of Ekron — who had thrown Padi — their king into fetters (because he was) loyal to (his) solemn oath (sworn) by the god Ashur, and had handed him over to Hezekiah the Jew (*Ha-za-qi-(i)a-u* ᵃᵐᵉˡ *Ia-u-da-ai*) (and) he (Hezekiah) held him in prison, unlawfully, as if he (Padi) be an enemy — had become afraid and had called (for help) upon the kings of Egypt (*Muṣ(u)ri*) (and) the bowmen, the chariot (corps) and the cavalry of the king of Ethiopia (*Meluhha*), an army beyond counting — and they (actually) had come to their assistance.[43]

After claiming a victory at Eltekeh over the opposition, Sennacherib continues:

> As to Hezekiah, the Jew, he did not submit to my yoke, I laid siege to 46 of his strong cities, walled forts and to the countless small villages in their vicinity, and conquered (them) by means of well-stamped (earth-) ramps, and battering-rams brought (thus) near (to the walls) (combined with) the attack by foot soldiers, (using) mines, breeches as well as sapper work. I drove out (of them) 200,150 people, young and old, male and female, horses, mules, donkeys, camels, big and small cattle beyond counting, considered (them) booty. Himself I made a prisoner in Jerusalem, his royal residence, like a bird in a cage. I surrounded him with earthwork in order to molest those who were leaving his city's gate. His towns which I had plundered, I took away from his country and gave them (over) to Mitinti, king of Ashdod, Padi, king of Ekron, and Sillibel, king of Gaza. Thus I reduced his country, but I still increased the tribute and the *katru*-presents (due) to me (as his) overlord which I imposed (later) upon him beyond the former tribute, to be delivered annually. Hezekiah himself, whom the terror-inspiring splendor of my lordship had overwhelmed and whose irregular and elite troops which he had brought into Jerusalem his royal residence, in order to strengthen (it), had deserted him, did send me, later, to Nineveh, my lordly city, together with 30 talents of gold, 800 talents of silver, precious stones, antimony, large cuts of red stone, couches (inlaid) with ivory, *nimedu*-chairs (inlaid) with ivory, elephant-hides, ebony-wood, boxwood (and) all kinds of valuable treasures, his own daughters, concubines, male and female musicians. In order to deliver the tribute and to do obeisance as a slave he sent his (personal) messenger.[44]

---

43 *ANET*, p. 287.
44 *Ibid.*, p. 288.

The account of the tribute in this Annal, while agreeing on the amount of gold — 30 talents — lists eight hundred talents of silver contrasted with the three hundred of silver listed in the Bible (II Kings 18:14). The Bible is also silent on the additional items which Sennacherib maintains were paid.

In addition to the above Annal, other notices of the invasion are to be found. Sennacherib in the "Bull Inscription" relates:

> I laid waste the large district of Judah (*Ia-u-di*) and made the overbearing and proud Hezekiah (*Ha-za-qi-a-a-a*) its king, bow in submission.[45]
>
> Yet a third source, the Nebi Yunus slab, claims: I laid waste the large district of Judah and put the straps of my (yoke) upon Hezekiah, its king.[46]

Sennacherib does not discuss the destruction of his army nor anything of the circumstances under which he withdrew from Judah.

Shebna

Shebna, prime minister ("who is over the house") of Judah under Hezekiah, was roundly denounced by Isaiah for carving for himself a tomb (Isa. 22:15-25). Isaiah threatens that Shebna will be cast from his place and that he will be replaced by Eliakim the son of Hilkiah. The threat seems to have come to a reality, for in 701 B.C. when the Judean representatives go out to parley with the Rabshakeh of Sennacherib, Hilkiah is "over the house"; whereas Shebna is "the secretary" (Isa. 36:3, 11, 22; 37:2; II Kings 18:18, 26, 37; 19:2).

A defective tomb inscription, now in the British Museum but found in the village of Silvan, describes the owner as "[. . .] *yahu* who is over the house." It has been conjectured by Avigad that the name should be restored as *Shebanyahu*.[47] The inscription dates from Hezekiah's period, and the correspondence in the title of its owner with that of Hezekiah's official is identical. Nevertheless, this conjecture should be recognized as merely that — a conjecture — and should not come to be considered a certainty by the mere process of multiple repetition.

---

45 *Ibid.*
46 *Ibid.*
47 "The Epitaph of a Royal Steward from Siloam Village," *IEJ*, III (1953), 137-152.

Manasseh

Hezekiah was succeeded on the throne of Judah by his son Manasseh. Manasseh's long reign of fifty-five years (*ca.* 687-642 B.C.) reversed the reforms of his father and fostered human sacrifice and the cult of the host of heaven. The Bible devotes more space to this aspect of his reign than to any other. The historian passes his most severe denunciation on this king (II Kings 21:1-18; II Chron. 33:1-20). The writer of Chronicles relates that at one stage in his career the commanders of Assyria carried Manasseh with hooks and bound him with fetters of bronze and brought him to Babylon (II Chron. 33:11). Upon his return he fortified the city of David and put army commanders in the fortified cities of Judah (II Chron. 33:14).

None of these matters are elsewhere recorded. However, among a list of twenty-two kings in the west who paid tribute to Esarhaddon and to Ashurbanipal we find the name of Manasseh.

Esarhaddon on Prism B lists those who contributed materials toward his new palace at Nineveh. He says,

> I called up the kings of the country Hatti and (of the region) on the other side of the (Euphrates)(to wit): Ba'lu, king of Tyre, Manasseh (*Me-na-si-i*) king of Judah (*Ia-ú-di*).[48]

Ashurbanipal on Cylinder C, which is composed of various fragments, reports of kings who were forced to accompany him "with their forces and their ships" in his Egyptian campaign against Thebes in 663 B.C. Among these kings were:

> Ba'al, king of Tyre, Manasseh (*Mi-in-si-e*) king of Judah (*Ia-ú-di*).[49]

Jehoiachin

Following the death of Jehoiachim, his son Jehoiachin ascended to the throne for a brief time, but after three months surrendered the city of Jerusalem to Nebuchadnezzar. A Babylonian account of the fall of the city establishes its date as March 15/16, 597 B.C.:

> In the seventh year, the month of Kislev, the king of Akkad mustered his troups, marched to Hatti-land, and encamped against (i.e., besieged) the city of Judah and on the second

---

48 *ANET*, p. 291.
49 *Ibid.*, p. 294; Schrader, *op. cit.*, II, 39-43.

day of the month of Adar he seized the city and captured the king. He appointed there a king of his own choice (lit.: heart), received its heavy tribute and sent (them) to Babylon.[50]

Jehoiachin and important Judean figures, including the prophet Ezekiel, were taken into exile, and Zedekiah was appointed king (II Kings 24:10-17).

After thirty-seven years had passed by, Jehoiachin was freed from prison by Evil-Merodach when the latter came to the throne. The Judean king was appointed a place at the king's table with other captive kings. In this status he continued until his death (II Kings 25:27-30; Jer. 52:31-34).

Excavations in Babylon of a vaulted building near the Ishtar Gate revealed administrative documents, four of which give rations for captives, among whom are Jehoiachin and his sons.

---

50 D. J. Wiseman, *Chronicles of Chaldean Kings* (London: British Museum, 1956), p. 73.

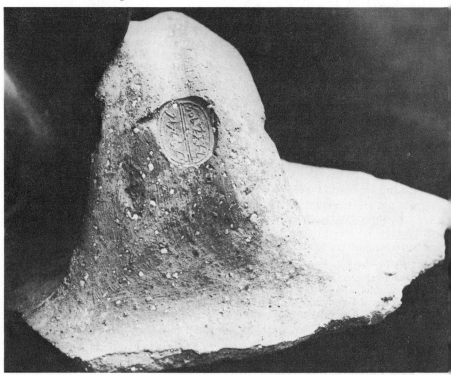

16. SEAL IMPRESSION ON THE JAR HANDLE from Tell Beit Mirsim. The seal is that of the steward of the Judean king Jehoiachin. Courtesy, Matson Photo Service

10 (sila of oil) to Iakuu'kinu son of the king of Iakudin. 2½ sila for the 5 sons of the king of Judah (*Iahudu*) through Qana'a.[51]

In excavations of Palestinian cities four jar handle stamp seals of officials of Jehoiachin have come to light from three different sites:

(a) Beth Shemish.
    "Belonging to Eliakim, steward of Yaukin."[52]

(b) Tell Beit Mirsim.
    In 1928 a jar handle was found by Albright impressed with "To Eliakim, Steward of Joiachin." In 1930 a second example was found. These two handles and the Beth Shemish example belong to the late post exilic age, are identical, and come from the same stamp.[53]

(c) Ramat Rahel.
    A seal: "Elyaqim, Steward of Yaukin."[54]

Studies of this type of Palestinian seal establish that they tend to be those of royal officials. There is every reason to identify Yaukin of the seals with the king of Judah.

Gedaliah

Following the capitulation of Jerusalem (586 B.C.) and the exiling of the captives, Nebuchadnezzar chose Gedaliah, son of Ahikam, son of Shaphan, to govern the people who remained in the land of Judea. Gedaliah's father had protected Jeremiah when the people would have slain him (Jer. 26:24). Gedaliah's short lived government centered at Mizpah rather than at Jerusalem. Two months after the burning of the temple, Gedaliah, having ignored warnings that his life was in danger, was assassinated by Ishmael (II Kings 25:22-26; Jer. 40:5—41:8).

In the excavation of Tell ed-Duweir (Lachish) a stamped jar

---

51 *ANET*, p. 308; E. F. Weidner, "Jojachin, König von Juda im babylonischen keilschrifttexten," *Mélanges syriens offerts à Monsieur René Dussaud* (Paris: Librairie Orientaliste Paul Geuthner, 1939), II, 923-935; W. F. Albright, "King Joiachin in Exile," *BA*, V (1942), 49-55.

52 Elihu Grant and G. Ernest Wright, *Ain Shems Excavations*, Pt. V ("Biblical and Kindred Studies," No. 3; Haverford: Haverford College, 1939), p. 80.

53 W. F. Albright, "The Seal of Eliakim and the Latest Preexilic History of Judah with some observations on Ezekiel," *JBL*, LI (1932), 77-106.

54 Y. Aharoni, *Excavations at Ramat Rahel* (Rome: Universita Degli Studi Centro Di Studi Semitici, 1962), pp. 59-60.

handle was discovered reading "Gedaliah who is over the house."
Though there cannot be absolute certainty, it was proposed by
Starkey and Hooke and accepted by many others that the man
whose name is on the seal is the same man as Nebuchadnezzar's
governor.[55]

Jaazaniah

After the fall of Jerusalem in 586 b.c. when the captains in
the open country (sare ha-hayalim) heard that Nebuchadnezzar
had appointed Gedaliah governor, they came to Mizpah to
Gedaliah and were advised by him to serve the king of Babylon. Among these was Jaazaniah the son of the Maacathite
(II Kings 25:23; Jer. 40:8). Three other men in the Bible at the
end of the Judean Kingdom bear the name Jaazaniah, but none
of them are connected with Mizpah: In Jerusalem there was a
Jaazaniah, the son of Jeremiah (not the prophet) who was one
of the house of the Rechabites (Jer. 35:3); there was a Jaazaniah, the son of Azzur (Ezek. 11:1); and in Babylon there was
a Jaazaniah, the son of Shaphan (Ezek. 8:11). One of the Lachish ostraca (1:3) has yet another Jaazaniah of this period. He
is Hobab ben Ya'zanyahu.[56]

In the excavation of Tell en-Nashbeh, on April 22, 1932, an
agate seal perforated to receive a carrying cord and bearing the
name of a Jaazaniah was uncovered in a tomb which had been
reused in the Christian period but which still had some remains
in it from the late Iron age. The tomb was number 19 and
was in the west necropolis of the tell. Tell en-Nashbeh is widely
identified with Mizpah, and it has been conjectured by the pub-
lisher of the seal, though there can never be certainty, that the
owner of the seal and the Biblical figure are one and the same
person. The Biblical Jaazaniah was an official (sar ha-hayalim)
and was connected with Mizpah. The owner of the seal was a
royal official, and if Tell en-Nashbeh is indeed Mizpah, there are
two striking points of contact.

The seal belongs to the beginning of the sixth century b.c. and

---

55 S. H. Hooke, "A Scarab and Sealing from Tell Duweir," PEFQS
(1935), 195-196; J. L. Starkey, "Lachish as Illustrating Bible History,"
PEFQS (1937), 173-174; David Diringer, "Early Hebrew Inscriptions," in
Olga Tufnell, Lachish (London: Oxford University Press, 1953), III,
348; L. R. de Vaux, "Le Sceau de Godolias, Maitre du Palais," RB, XLV
(1936), 96-102.

56 H. Torczyner, The Lachish Letters (London: Oxford University
Press, 1938), I, 23, 26.

has a representation of a cock — the earliest known from Palestine — and also has the Hebrew inscription clearly cut:

"To Jaazaniah, steward of the King."[57]

SUMMARY

With the setting in of the exile we bring this section of our study to an end. It has revealed information on seven kings of Israel: Omri, Jehu, Jehoash, Jeroboam II, Menahem, Pekah, and Hoshea. There are also six kings of Judah: Uzziah, Jotham, Ahaz, Hezekiah, Manasseh, and Jehoiachin. To these are to be added the governor Gedaliah and the official Jaazaniah, who are probably the figures on the seals mentioned earlier. Information about Shebna, on the other hand, is too doubtful for any assertions to be made.

To the accumulating total of men of the entire study Israel and Judah contribute fifteen figures.

---

57 W. F. Badè, "The Seal of Jaazaniah," ZAW, LI (1933), 150-156; C. C. McCowan, *Tell en-Nashbeh* (New Haven: American Schools of Oriental Research, 1947), I, 163.

VI

THE PERSIAN PERIOD

Our study of the men of the Persian period presents numerous difficulties. Some of these arise from the nature of Persian history itself, for Persia lacks a chronicler of her own. Though there are some sparse inscriptions, we derive our information about her chiefly from the Biblical writers, and from Herodotus, Xenophon, and other Greeks. Herodotus publicly recited his history in Athens in 445 B.C. (the year of Nehemiah's return to Jerusalem) and was rewarded for it.[1] But though contemporaries or near contemporaries of the events with which we are concerned, these figures — both Jews and Greeks — were foreigners, were Persia's national enemies and are hardly to be classified as objective witnesses.

The Old Testament mentions activities of at least four Persian kings. Because of the reports of the classical historians, there has never been any doubt about the existence of these figures. More recently their palaces and tombs have been excavated or identified.

However, in this most important period of Biblical history, none of the Old Testament episodes involving these Persian kings, except their conquering of Babylon and their sequence in office, is directly mentioned either in their known inscriptions or by the classical historians. It is widely recognized that the Biblical books dealing with the Persian period reflect a knowledge of Persian customs and culture. Policies parallel to Cyrus' decree permitting the return from exile can be cited from his cylinder, and literary style parallel to the Aramaic royal decrees of the book of Ezra can be claimed, but the researcher has to

---

1 A. T. Olmstead, *History of the Persian Empire* (Chicago: University of Chicago Press, 1948), p. 317.

content himself with these more remote contacts between the Biblical story and discovery. Individual details of these Biblical books continue to be a battleground.

The Biblical account of the Persian period also furnishes us numerous otherwise unknown personages. Some of these offer considerable historical difficulties such as the identities of Darius the Mede (Dan. 5:31) and of Ahasuerus the father of Darius the Mede (Dan. 9:1). It is to the first of these that we now turn attention.

DARIUS THE MEDE

The identity of Darius the Mede is one of the most perplexing problems of Old Testament study. This figure, the son of Ahasuerus (Dan. 9:1), is said to have received the kingdom at the age of sixty-two following the death of Belshazzar (Dan. 5:30-31). Darius proceeded to divide the kingdom into a hundred and twenty satrapies over one of which Daniel was appointed head (Dan. 6:1). It was also he who threw Daniel into the lion's den (Dan. 6:1-28). Daniel dates two of his visions in the first year of this Darius who was made king over the realm of the Chaldeans (Dan. 9:1; 11:1). It would appear that Darius was succeeded by Cyrus the Persian (Dan. 6:28).

Josephus vaguely identified Darius as a relative of Cyrus and remarks, "he was a son of Asytages but is called by another name among the Greeks,"[2] but Josephus does not tell us what the name was, and his case would not be accepted by modern scholars.

Darius has been the subject of limitless discussion, and within the present generation book-length studies have been devoted to him by H. H. Rowley and by J. C. Whitcomb, Jr. Rowley argues that no known candidate fits the qualifications needed and declares that Darius is a fictitious character.[3] He reaches a conclusion quite adverse to the historicity of the book of Daniel. Whitcomb, on the other hand, argues that Darius was an honorific title given to Gubaru, a subordinate official whom Cyrus had placed over Babylon. Taking exception to the popular rendering of the *Nabonidus Chronicle*, while following the translation of Sidney Smith, Whitcomb finds evidence for Gubaru in the *Chronicle* and certain other texts. He carefully distinguishes Gubaru from Gobryas, who was suggested by earlier studies

2 *Ant.* x. 11. 4 (248-249).
3 *Darius the Mede and the Four World Empires in the Book of Daniel* (Cardiff: University of Wales Press, 1959), 195 pp.

based on references in the Behistun inscription and the classical historians. Whitcomb has to grant that no cuneiform text gives Gubaru's father's name, his nationality, specifically calls him a king, or calls him Darius.[4] At the best the case opens a possibility but cannot be considered a certainty.

The question of Darius still remains unanswered. Both secular history and archaeological discovery know of no one ruling in Babylon between Belshazzar and Cyrus the Great. We do not have material on Darius the Mede or upon his father Ahasuerus. We do not know who he was or how he fits into the picture of history to be learned from non-Biblical sources.

CYRUS

Isaiah pointed to Cyrus as the Lord's shepherd and anointed, raised up and given success at every stage in order to bring to an end the exile and to bring about the building of the temple (Isa. 44:28—45:3). It was Cyrus whose hand the Lord had grasped and whom he had called by name though Cyrus knew not the Lord. There is little reason to assume validity in Josephus' story that Cyrus was stimulated to action by having read Isaiah.[5]

In this first year (538 B.C.) Cyrus made a decree that the exiles could go up to Jerusalem and build the temple:

> The Lord, the God of heaven, has given me all the kingdoms of the earth, and he has charged me to build him a house at Jerusalem, which is in Judah. Whoever is among you of all his people, may his God be with him, and let him go up to Jerusalem, which is in Judah, and rebuild the house of the Lord, the God of Israel — he is the God who is in Jerusalem; and let each survivor, in whatever place he sojourns, be assisted by the men of his place with silver and gold, with goods and with beasts, besides freewill offerings for the house of God which is in Jerusalem (Ezra 1:2-4).

Both Chronicles (II Chron. 36:23) and Ezra cite this decree and a search of the archives of Ecbatana by Darius during his reign revealed a copy there (Ezra 6:3-5). Cyrus also brought forth the vessels that had been taken from the temple and entrusted them to Sheshbazzar to return them to Jerusalem.

---

4 *Darius the Mede* (Grand Rapids: Eerdmans, 1959), 84 pp.; R. K. Harrison, *Introduction to the Old Testament*, Grand Rapids: Eerdmans, 1969), pp. 342-343, points out that Rowley's case is largely vitiated by his dependence upon inaccurate or unreliable secondary sources.

5 *Ant.* xi. 1. 2 (5-6).

The result was the first return from exile and the establishment of the post-exilic community led by Zerubbabel and Jeshua. Cyrus' grant also gave the right to bring cedar from Lebanon for the purpose of building (Ezra 3:7). Already, however, in the time of Cyrus, opposition was encountered from the people of the land frustrating the building of the temple until the time of Darius (Ezra 4:4-5).

Some people, taken into exile by Nebuchadnezzar, lived out the exile into the reign of Cyrus. One of these was Daniel (Dan. 1:21; 6:28), who dates one of his visions in the third year of Cyrus (Dan. 10:1).

The career of Cyrus can be traced from Herodotus,[6] Xenophon,[7] the *Nabonidus Chronicle*[8] and the *Persian Verse Account*.[9] Beginning as king of Anshan, *ca.* 549 B.C., Cyrus extended his territory to include Media; he then defeated Croesus, king of Lydia (546 B.C.);[10] and his general Harpagus defeated also the Greek states of Asia Minor in the following year. Cyrus began his attack on Nabonidus and Babylon in 539 B.C. After taking Opis and Sippar, according to the *Chronicle,* his troops led by Gobryas, governor of Gutium, entered Babylon without a battle on October 13, 539 B.C.[11] Shortly thereafter Nabonidus was arrested,[12] and on October 29, sixteen days after the capitulation, Cyrus entered the city. With the conquest of Egypt by Cambyses in 525 B.C. the Persians had in thirty years extended their territory over a larger area than that reigned over by any of the monarchs of the Mesopotamian or Nile Valleys. This empire was maintained within one family for two centuries.[13]

No records of Cyrus directly parallel any Biblical event or speak specifically of the Jews. Persian records engage in a great deal of propagandizing to justify Cyrus' seizure of Babylon and at the same time they villainize Nabonidus. In the well-known Cyrus cylinder, Cyrus gives Marduk credit for having chosen him and having exalted him to his position:

---

6 *Histories* i. 95-216.

7 *Cyropaedia* viii. 5. 1-36; etc.

8 *ANET,* pp. 305-306; D. W. Thomas, *Documents from Old Testament Times* (London: Nelson, 1951), pp. 82-83.

9 *ANET,* pp. 313-315.

10 Herodotus *Histories* i. 79 ff.; 83 ff.; Xenophon *Cyropaedia* vii. 2. 1 ff.; *Nabonidus Chronicle* ii. 16-18.

11 *ANET,* p. 306.

12 *Ibid.*

13 G. B. Gray, "The Foundation and Extension of the Persian Empire," *CAH,* IV, 62.

He scanned and looked (through) all the countries, searching for a righteous ruler willing to lead him (*i.e.*, Marduk) (in the annual procession). (Then) he pronounced the name of Cyrus, king of Anshan, declared him (lit.: pronounced [his] name) to be(come) the ruler of all the world.[14]

A text found at Ur, in contrast, gives Sin the moon-god credit for Cyrus' victories.[15] Cyrus states that he was welcomed by the people of Babylon as he entered Babylon as a friend and that he brought blessings to the city.

On the cylinder Cyrus proceeded to proclaim himself king:

I am Cyrus, king of the world, great king, legitimate king, king of Babylon, king of Sumer and Akkad, king of the four rims (of the earth), son of Cambyses, great king, king of Anshan, grandson of Cyrus, great king, king of Anshan, descendant of Teispes, great king, king of Anshan, of a family (which) always (exercised) kingship whose rule Bel and Nebo love whom they want as king to please their hearts.[16]

---

14 *ANET*, p. 315.
15 Thomas, *op. cit.*, p. 94, notes.
16 *ANET*, p. 316.

17. THE CYRUS CYLINDER in which the Persian king describes his policy toward captive peoples. Courtesy, British Museum

Of greatest interest to Old Testament students is Cyrus' announcement that it was his policy that the sanctuaries of subject peoples could be restored:

> (As to the region) from . . . as far as Ashur and Susa, Agade, Eshnunna, the towns of Zamban, Mo-Turnu, Der as well as the region of the Gutians, I returned to (these) sacred cities on the other side of the Tigris, the sanctuaries of which have been ruins for a long time, the images which (used) to live therein and established for them permanent sanctuaries. I (also) gathered all their (former) inhabitants and returned (to them) their habitations. Furthermore, I resettled upon the command of Marduk the great lord, all the gods of Sumer and Akkad whom Nabonidus has brought into Babylon (Su.an.na-^{ki}) to the anger of the lord of the gods, unharmed, in their (former) chapels, the places which made them happy.
> May all the gods whom I have resettled in their sacred cities ask daily Bel and Nebo for long life for me and may they recommend me (to him); to Marduk, my lord, they may say thus: "Cyrus, the king who worships you, and Cambyses, his son, . . ." . . . all of them I settled in a peaceful place.[17]

Cyrus' palace, built at Pasargadae, has inscriptions which at least five times proclaim: "I am Cyrus, the king of the Achaemenid."[18] Cyrus died on a campaign against the nomads on the eastern edge of the empire.[19] His tomb, which was rifled in the time of Alexander the Great, is a structure built of square cut limestone containing an interior chamber for the body.[20] Its inscription reads:

> O man, whosoever thou art and whencesoever thou comest, for I know that thou wilt come, I am Cyrus, and I won the Persians their empire. Do not, therefore, begrudge me this little earth which covers my body![21]

DARIUS

Cambyses, son and successor to Cyrus on the throne of Persia, is passed over in complete silence in the Old Testament despite his extending the empire to include Egypt in 525 B.C. Darius, on

17 Ibid.
18 R. N. Frye, The Heritage of Persia (Cleveland: World Publishing Co., 1963), p. 80.
19 Gray, op. cit., IV, 15.
20 ANEP, No. 768; G. B. Gray and M. Cary, "The reign of Darius," CAH, IV, 189.
21 Plutarch Life of Alexander lxix. 2 (LCL, VII, 417); cf. Arrian Anabasis of Alexander vi. 29. 5 (LCL, II, 197).

the other hand, who came to the throne following the untimely death of Cambyses, plays a significant part in the rebuilding of the temple.

Both Haggai and Zechariah, who have major roles in stimulating the returned exiles to complete the temple, date their oracles in the second year (520 B.C.) of Darius (Haggai 1:1; Zech. 1:1). People of Bethel later raise a question in his fourth year concerning the propriety of continuing traditional fasts (Zech. 7:1).

Work on the temple had been in a state of frustration since objections to it had been raised in the reign of Cyrus (Ezra 4:5, 24). Stimulated by the prophets, the people began rebuilding (Ezra 5:1 ff.). New letters were sent to Darius from Tattenai, governor of Beyond the River, and his associates. At the behest of Darius, search disclosed a copy of Cyrus' decree in Ecbatana, resulting in a fourth decree of Darius that not only was no hindrance to be put in the way, but positive aid was to be given "that they . . . may pray for the life of the king and his sons" (Ezra 6:1 ff.). The final result was that the temple was completed and dedicated in the sixth year of Darius (516 B.C.) (Ezra 6:15 ff.). This much we learn from the Old Testament.

Following the death of Cambyses, Darius, son of Hystaspes, a Persian prince from the other line, seized the throne (522-486 B.C.) despite great opposition. His successful overcoming of opposition is commemorated in the well-known Behistun trilingual (Old Persian, Elamite, and Akkadian) inscription in the mountains between Kermanshah and Hamadan, Iran, which, when deciphered by Henry Rawlinson in the last century, furnished the key to unlocking cuneiform writing.[22] Darius depicts himself treading on the neck of the leader of the opposition and tells of his struggles for the throne.[23] The inscription is the most considerable piece of literature surviving in old Persian and is of great importance as an original historical document.[24] Fragments of an Aramaic version have been found in Egypt,[25] and fragments of an Akkadian version from Babylon are also known.[26] Praising Ahuramazda as a great god, Darius

---

22 Rawlinson's description of his activity is reprinted in Leo Deuel, *The Treasures of Time* (London: Pan Books, 1964), pp. 126-130.

23 *ANEP*, Nos. 249, 462.

24 J. H. Iliffe, "Persia and the Ancient World," *The Legacy of Persia*, ed. A. J. Arberry (Oxford: Clarendon Press, 1953), p. 20.

25 A. E. Cowley, *Aramaic Papyri of the Fifth Century B.C.* (Oxford: Clarendon Press, 1923), pp. 248-271.

26 Olmstead, *op. cit.*, p. 116.

insists, "I am a friend to the right, I am not a friend to wrong."[27]

The earliest of the Elephantine papyri is dated by the regnal years of Darius.[28] His activities are surveyed by the classical historians, to some extent by his own inscriptions, and by business and administrative documents dated in his reign.[29]

Darius attempted unsuccessfully to put down a revolt in the Greek states and met defeat at the famous battle of Marathon in 490 B.C. Darius erected a palace at Susa[30] extensive remains of which have been excavated by the French, who also found a text which relates how Darius carried out the work.[31] Cuneiform texts from this locale tell of building activities of Darius, Xerxes, Artaxerxes I, and their successors.[32] It was Darius also who constructed a palace at Persepolis (512-494 B.C.) which had the inscription: "I am Darius, great king, king of kings, king of lands, son of Hystaspes, the Achaemenid, who constructed this palace."[33] On one of the gate jambs Darius is shown on his throne with Xerxes the crown prince standing behind him.[34] In this city also have been found the royal archives chiefly written in Elamite.[35]

In Egypt Darius continued work on the canal connecting the Red Sea and the Nile, a project which had been begun by Pharaoh Necho. Fragments of an inscription commemorating this event have been found.[36] A cylinder seal (BM 89132) discovered in Egypt shows the king hunting a lion from his chariot and it is inscribed in three languages: "Darius the Great King." The seal possibly belonged to Darius I, though some scholars attribute it to his son.[37]

The tomb of Darius I at Naqsh-i-Rustam, northeast of Persepolis, has a trilingual inscription in which he describes his character and accomplishments.[38] Strabo affirms that a Greek

---

27 R. G. Kent, "Old Persian Texts," *JNES*, IV (1945), 39-52.

28 Cowley, *op. cit.*, No. 1.

29 *ANET*, pp. 221, K, No. 3, 316, No. 4.

30 Olmstead, *op. cit.*, pp. 168 ff.

31 R. Ghirshman, *Iran* (Baltimore: Penguin Books, 1961), pp. 165-166.

32 Frye, *op. cit.*, p. 95.

33 J. Finegan, *Light from the Ancient Past* (Princeton: Princeton University Press, 1959), p. 241.

34 *ANEP*, No. 463.

35 Olmstead, *op. cit.*, pp. 176 ff.

36 Frye, *op. cit.*, p. 107; Gray and Cary, *op. cit.*, IV, 200; Olmstead, *op. cit.*, p. 146; cf. Herodotus *Histories* ii. 158; Diodorus Siculus *Library of History* i. 33. 9.

37 R. D. Barnett, *Illustrations of Old Testament History* (London: British Museum, 1966), p. 78.

38 *ANEP*, No. 769; Kent, *op. cit.*, pp. 39-52.

version of the inscription reads:

> I was a friend to my friends; as a horseman and bowman I
> proved myself superior to all others; as hunter I prevailed; I
> could do everything.[39]

Like the records for Cyrus, the records concerning Darius,
Xerxes, and Artaxerxes do not directly pertain to the information
given concerning them in the Bible.

AHASUERUS

The people of the land who frustrated the rebuilding of the
temple during the reign of Cyrus until the reign of Darius (Ezra
4:4-5) are also said to have written an accusation in the reign
of Ahasuerus (Ezra 4:6). It is to be noticed in this section of
Ezra that the reign of Ahasuerus is mentioned between that of
Cyrus (Ezra 4:5) and that of Artaxerxes (Ezra 4:7).

Ahasuerus is met prominently in the book of Esther where he
is said to have reigned from India to Ethiopia over 127 provinces
and to have had his capital in Susa. His famous banquet in
which he chose to display the beauty of his queen Vashti came
in his third year (Esther 1:3). Vashti's refusal to appear brought
her downfall. In her place, out of all the beautiful candidates,
Hadassah (Esther) was chosen in the seventh year (Esther
2:16 ff.) and succeeded in gaining the king's favor. Haman's
animosity toward the Jews, now overplayed in the planning of a
pogrom throughout Persia, gave Esther her opportunity to deliver her people by interceding with the king. As a result of
her intercession, Haman was hanged, the Jews of Persia overcame
their enemies, Mordecai was exalted to a place next to Ahasuerus, and the feast of Purim had its origin.

Despite the fact that the honors accorded to Mordecai are
said to have been written in the chronicles of the kings of Media
and Persia, the characters of the book of Esther: Vashti, Esther,
and Haman are as of this date otherwise unknown to history.
It has been convincingly argued that Ahasuerus is to be identified with Xerxes, son of Darius, who occupied the throne 486-
465 B.C.[40] The Persian name *Khshayarsha* becomes *Ahashwe-
rosh* in Hebrew, *Assoueros* or *Xerxes* in Greek, and *Assuerus* in
Latin from which form comes the name *Ahasuerus* followed in
the English Bibles.

---

39 Strabo *Geography* xv. 3. 8.
40 Josephus *Ant.* xi. 6. 1 (184), identifies Ahasuerus with Artaxerxes
which identification he obtains from a reading of LXX.

18. PERSEPOLIS RELIEF showing Babylonians and Syrians bringing tribute to Darius. Courtesy, Oriental Institute

Xerxes was a son of Darius and his queen Atossa, the daughter of Cyrus the Great. His place on the throne in preference to his brothers was determined by Darius before the latter's death. A jamb on the middle palace door at Persepolis proclaimed him: "Xerxes, Darius the king's son, the Achaemenid."[41] He was able to make good his claim despite the rebellions that occurred at the beginning of his reign.[42] In the remains of the Council Hall

41 Olmstead, *op. cit.*, p. 227.
42 *ANET*, pp. 316-317.

at Persepolis Xerxes is depicted standing behind Darius who is seated on the throne.[43] The gate of Xerxes has the inscription:

> I am Xerxes, the great king, king of kings, king of the lands of many peoples, king of this great earth far and wide. By Ahuramazda's favor I made this gate "All Lands."[44]

Events of his reign are covered by Herodotus in Books VII-IX, by his own inscriptions, and by clay tablets from the archives at Persepolis.[45] Xerxes, a loyal worshipper of Ahuramazda, put down the false gods in his realm as an inscription of his from Persepolis reveals.[46]

Xerxes' authority in Egypt is attested by the discovery of trilingual seals and by vases inscribed, "Xerxes the great king."[47] Also a mercenary force at Elephantine is attested by the Aramaic papyri from that place, some of which are dated by his regnal years.[48]

Though the forces of Xerxes experienced initial success in the drive to subjugate Greece by overrunning Leonidas and his Spartans at Thermopylae in 480 B.C., the naval battle at Salamis in the same year ended in disaster. Shortly afterward a land battle at Plataea in 479 B.C. brought the withdrawal of the Persians from Greece. After this event, according to Herodotus, Xerxes sought solace in his harem.[49] Xerxes eventually met his death in 465 B.C. from poison administered by the hands of an assassin. His rock-hewn tomb, devoid of inscriptions, is at Naqsh-i-Rustam, east of that of Darius.[50]

The major question concerning Xerxes continues to be that of the historicity of the events related about him in the book of Esther. Recent defenses of the historicity of the book are to be found in the introductions to the Old Testament by E. J. Young,[51] G. L. Archer,[52] and R. K. Harrison;[52a] the opposite

---

43 *ANEP,* No. 463.
44 Olmstead, *op. cit.,* p. 285.
45 *Ibid.,* pp. 272 ff.
46 *ANET,* pp. 316-317.
47 G. Posener, *La premiére domination Perse en Égypte* (Le Caire: L'Institut Francais d'archéologie Orientale, 1936), Nos. 43-77.
48 Cowley, *op. cit.,* Nos. 2 & 5.
49 *Histories* ix. 108.
50 Olmstead, *op. cit.,* p. 289.
51 *An Introduction to the Old Testament* (Grand Rapids: Eerdmans, 1953), pp. 346-348.
52 *A Manual of Introduction to the Old Testament* (Chicago: Moody Press, 1964), pp. 404-406.
52a *Op. cit.,* pp. 1090-1092.

line is followed by Gottwald, Weiser, Eissfeldt, and others. One of the issues is that of the name of Xerxes' queen. According to Herodotus, the queen of Xerxes was Amestris, daughter of a Persian noble named Otanes.[53] Efforts of earlier apologists to identify her with Esther have been abandoned. More recent treatments of the question which uphold the historicity of the book point out that Herodotus fails to mention many important persons and events in his account; hence, it is not surprising that he passes over Biblical characters. Herodotus does mention that in his seventh year Xerxes, returning from his Greek defeat, sought consolation in his harem.[54] In the absence of evidence, it is conjectured that it is possible that at this time, doing as he pleased,[55] he chose a new queen. For a fuller treatment of the problems concerned with the historicity of the book of Esther the reader is referred to the above-mentioned sources.

ARTAXERXES

The opposition of the people of the land to the reconstruction of Jerusalem in the days of Artaxerxes finds expression in the Aramaic letter from Bishlam, Mithredath, and Tabeel in the name of Rehum the commander and Shimshai the scribe to Artaxerxes. These men informed the king of the progress of the work and warned that continuance would endanger the authority of the king in the province Beyond the River. The result was a decree from the king which prohibited further work, a decree put into effect by Rehum, Shimshai, and their associates (Ezra 4:7-23).

Ezra the scribe led this group of returnees to Jerusalem in the seventh year of Artaxerxes (Ezra 7:7). A letter from Artaxerxes authorized the return, the collection of freewill offerings to purchase sacrifices, and the supplying of additional money from the king's treasury as needed. Orders went out to the treasurers in the province Beyond the River to lend aid up to specified amounts and to grant exemptions from tax and toll to the priests and Levites in the project. Ezra was authorized to appoint magistrates and to teach the Law in Jerusalem (Ezra 7:11-26).

The activities of Nehemiah are first dated in the twentieth year of Artaxerxes. In Susa, Nehemiah learned from men who had come out of Judah of the state of the city (Neh. 1:1 ff.) and secured permission to go to Jerusalem for the purpose of repair-

---

53 *Histories* vii. 61, 114.
54 *Ibid.*, ix. 108.
55 *Ibid.*, iii. 31.

ing its fortifications (Neh. 2:1 ff.). Despite opposition of Sanballat, Tobiah, and Geshem, Nehemiah carried the project
through to completion in good time, and a public assembly was
held for the reading of the Law (Neh. 8:1 ff.). The feast of
booths was observed, and a public confession of sin was made
(Neh. 9:1 ff.). Nehemiah was back in Susa for an unknown
period of time which began in the thirty-second year of Artaxerxes (Neh. 13:6). Still later Nehemiah was back in Jerusalem and carried through reforms concerned with Sabbath
observance, mixed marriages, and temple service (Neh. 13:10-
31). How long this visit continued we do not know.

The question of the identity of Artaxerxes is complicated by
the fact that three Persian figures of this general period had that
name: Artaxerxes I, Longimanus (464-424 B.C.); Artaxerxes II,
Mnemon (404-359 B.C.), and Artaxerxes III, Ochus (359-338
B.C.). The brevity of this last reign eliminates Ochus from con-
sideration, but complicated arguments over the dates and relative order of Ezra and Nehemiah continue. The evidence of the
Elephantine papyri, dated in 408 B.C. (the seventeenth year of
Darius II), which mentions the names of Sanballat and Jonathan the high priest (cf. Neh. 2:19; 12:23), would seem to establish that Nehemiah was active in the reign of Artaxerxes I
and thus came to Jerusalem in 445 B.C. and returned to Susa in
432 B.C. If the Biblical order is to be maintained, then Ezra, who
precedes Nehemiah, would have returned in 457 B.C. There is
a widespread view, however, which reverses the order and argues that Ezra was active in the reign of Artaxerxes II; that is,
in 398 B.C. The argument is complicated, but its crux seems to
be that Jehohanan, son of Eliashib, is mentioned in connection
with the work of Ezra (Ezra 10:6). Since he is also mentioned
as being high priest in the Elephantine papyri, it is argued that
Ezra must be dated as a close contemporary with that material.
Those who wish to uphold the Biblical order deny the identity
of Jehohanan of Ezra 10:6 with the one of the papyri[56] or argue
that Scripture does not actually say that Jehohanan was high
priest when Ezra spent the night in his chamber (Ezra 10:6).
It is further argued that he was at that time a young man and
that he later became high priest as the Elephantine papyri imply.[57] Thereby it is concluded that Jehohanan could still be

---

56 P. Heinisch, *History of the Old Testament,* trans. W. G. Heidt (Col-
legeville, Minnesota: Liturgical Press, 1952), p. 331.
57 Cowley, *op. cit.,* No. 30; cf. Young, *op. cit.,* p. 375.

high priest a half century after Ezra's visit and that Ezra could precede Nehemiah during the reign of Artaxerxes I.

Artaxerxes I, son of Xerxes, is well known from the classical historians, from some of the Elephantine papyri which are dated by his regnal years,[58] and from the survey of his reign by Josephus, though the latter is not an independent witness for this part of Biblical history.

Early in his reign Artaxerxes completed his father's Hall of a Hundred Columns at Persepolis. By 461 B.C. he had moved to Susa[59] where he built a small palace at the southern edge of the city,[60] but near the close of his reign he returned to Persepolis.[61] He overcame unrest in Egypt whence examples of inscriptional occurrence of his name can be found,[62] and he entered into a treaty with Athens in 449 B.C.[63] Artaxerxes' tomb, carrying no inscription, is at Naqsh-i-Rustam beside, but west of, those of Xerxes and Darius.[64]

MORDECAI

In turning to the lesser figures of the Persian period, we first notice Mordecai, who plays a prominent role in the book of Esther. Mordecai, a Benjamite at the court of Ahasuerus, is the subject of vigorous debate because of the statement made in Esther 2:5-6 where four generations of names are listed. If the passage asserts — as is often assumed — that Mordecai was carried off by Nebuchadnezzar, then he must have been an old man of more than a hundred years by the time Xerxes ascended the throne.[65] It is unlikely that a man of such age would play the role assigned to Mordecai. If, on the other hand, the relative clause of the verse describes Kish, whose name is at the end of the list, as being carried off by Nebuchadnezzar,[66] there is no chronological problem.

Mordecai, who had reared Esther (Esther 2:7, 15), revealed

58 Cowley, op. cit., Nos. 6, 7, 8, 9, 10, 13, 14.
59 Herodotus Histories vii. 151; Olmstead, op. cit., p. 252.
60 Ghirshman, op. cit., p. 172.
61 Olmstead, op. cit., p. 352.
62 Ibid., p. 291.
63 Ibid., pp. 310-311.
64 ANEP, No. 769.
65 O. Eissfeldt, The Old Testament, trans. by P. R. Achroyd (New York: Harper and Row, 1965), p. 507; A. Weiser, The Old Testament: Its Formation and Development, trans. by D. M. Barton (New York: Association Press, 1961), p. 311; et alia.
66 Young, op. cit., pp. 346-347; and Archer, op. cit., p. 404.

a plot of the eunuchs against Ahasuerus, but at the time went unrewarded (Esther 2:21 ff.; 6:2). His refusal to show honor to Haman stirred up the unlimited animosity of the latter figure and set the stage for Haman's planned pogrom against the Jews (Esther 3:1 ff.; 5:9). At Mordecai's insistence Esther pled with the king and brought deliverance and vengeance for the Jews. Esther set Mordecai over the house of Haman and the king gave him his signet ring (Esther 8:1-2). He led his people in their revenge against their enemies and was next in rank to the king.

An undated cuneiform text (Amherst tablet #258) found at Borsippa reveals that a man named Mordecai (*Marduka*) was a finance officer of some sort at the court at Susa during the early days of Xerxes' reign. A. Ungnad has argued that it is very likely that this is the first and single extra-Biblical allusion to Mordecai — that it is unlikely that two officials named Mordecai would have been at the court of Xerxes.[67] While the impact of Ungnad's announcement does not seem widely reflected in many of the Old Testament handbooks currently in use, it cannot be dismissed.

At a later period when Judas Maccabeus defeated the Syrian armies of Nicanor, II Maccabees informs us that "Nicanor's day" is to be celebrated on the day before "Mordecai's day" (II Macc. 15:36). This allusion is, of course, not independent of the Biblical book, but is of importance in the history of the feast of Purim.

SANBALLAT

Major opposition to the work of Nehemiah in rebuilding the walls of Jerusalem was offered by Sanballat the Horonite, Tobiah the servant, the Ammonite, and Geshem the Arab. Displeased at hearing of Nehemiah's mission, they at first derided his work by accusing him of rebelling against the king (Neh. 2:10, 19). With the actual work under way Sanballat ridiculed by saying in the presence of his brethren and the army of Samaria, "What are these feeble Jews doing? Will they restore things? Will they sacrifice? Will they finish up in a day? Will they revive the stones out of the heaps of rubbish, and burned ones at that?" (Neh. 4:2).

Such opposition proved ineffective; hence the three next

---

67 "Keilinschriftliche Beiträge zum Buch Ezra und Ester," ZAW, LVIII (1940/41), 240-244; LIX (1942/43), 219; S. H. Horn, "Mordecai, A Historical Problem," *Biblical Research,* IX (1964), 14-25.

plotted, again ineffectively, to come and fight against Jerusalem and to cause confusion in it (Neh. 4:7-9).

Once the breaches of the wall had been stopped, the three proposed a meeting in one of the villages of the plain of Ono; but Nehemiah, sensing their plan to dispose of him, rejected the invitation (Neh. 6:2). A letter from Sanballat accusing Nehemiah of plans to revolt was Sanballat's fifth contact with Nehemiah (Neh. 6:5). Next he hired Shemaiah, son of Delaiah, to warn Nehemiah that his life was in danger, hoping that Nehemiah would lose face by flight (Neh. 6:10-14). Nehemiah refused to fall victim to any of these stratagems. His final conflict with his opponent was during his second term in Jerusalem while carrying through the marriage reform. One of the sons of Jehoiada, the son of Eliashib the high priest, was the son-in-law of Sanballat the Horonite. Nehemiah proceeded to chase him away (Neh. 13:28).

It is likely, as we have seen earlier, that Nehemiah's career fell in the reign of Artaxerxes I (464-424 B.C.). His first trip is therefore to be dated in 445 B.C. (the twentieth year of Artaxerxes; cf. Neh. 1:1; 2:1), and his second trip sometime after the thirty-second year of Artaxerxes; that is, after 432 B.C.

The home of Sanballat was likely one of the Beth Horons, from which he is called the Horonite. Located at the edge of the Mediterranean plain and the hill region, these two towns controlled the road from Jerusalem to the coast.

Josephus, in surveying this period, supposes that Manasses, brother of Jaddus [Jaddua], was the son-in-law of Sanaballetes [Sanballat].[68] Josephus further has the elders of Jerusalem offering to Manasses the choice of divorce or expulsion from his priestly privilege. Sanballat retaliated by building the temple on Mt. Gerizim and establishing Manasses in the priesthood there.[69] The whole affair is set in the reign of Darius III (338-331 B.C.) and is related as a prelude to Josephus' account of Alexander the Great's visit to Jerusalem. Josephus relates how Sanballat visited Alexander during the siege of Tyre and obtained his permission to build the temple.[70]

The discovery of material in the Elephantine papyri dealing with Sanballat made completely unacceptable the case of those who favored Josephus' chronology to that of Nehemiah. The

---

68 *Ant.* xi. 7. 2 (302-303).
69 *Ibid.,* xi. 8. 2 (306-312).
70 *Ibid.,* xi. 8. 4 (321-322).

Aramaic letter of the priests of Elephantine dated in 407 B.C. and addressed to Bagoas, governor of Judah, which requests aid in rebuilding the temple at Elephantine, concluded:

> We have also set the whole matter forth in a letter in our name to Delaiah and Shelemiah, the sons of Sanballat, the governor of Samaria.[71]

Nehemiah does not call Sanballat "governor of Samaria," but if Sanballat were a mature man in 445 B.C. as implied in Nehemiah, it is to be expected that his sons would have taken over by 407 B.C. as seems to be implied in the papyrus letter.

The unusual discovery in 1962 by Bedouins of papyrus scrolls in the Wadi Daliyeh, fourteen kilometers north of Jericho, puts new factors into the discussion. These scrolls dating in the fourth century B.C. (375 B.C. to 335 B.C.) conjectured to have been hidden by the Samaritans at the threat of Alexander the Great's invasion of the Middle East, represent fragments of about forty documents only twenty of which are of any appreciable extent. Though these are as yet unpublished, their editor reports that the name "Sanballat" [Sin'uballit] occurs twice, once on an official sealing in Palaeo-Hebrew script and once in Aramaic in the text of one of the documents.[72] The figure spoken of in each is identified as "son of Sanballat."

It is conjectured that there may have been a sequence of three Sanballats holding governorship at intervals in Samaria. The first is met in Nehemiah and in the Elephantine materials; the second in the Wadi Daliyeh materials; and the third is described by Josephus. Delaiah, son of Sanballat, and Hananiah, son of Sanballat, intervene in the list of governors. Frank Cross, the editor, calls attention to the fact that other examples of pappyonymy — naming a child for his grandfather — are to be seen in this period: in the Tobiad family for nine generations and in the high priestly family in Judah where the names Onias and Simon alternate for five generations.

This of course involves assuming a chronological error on Josephus' part. In identifying the Biblical Sanballat with Sanballat III (assuming Cross' case) Josephus jumped from the

---

71 *ANET,* p. 492.

72 F. M. Cross, "The Discovery of the Samaria Papyri," *BA,* XXVI (1963), 110-121: "Aspects of Samaritan and Jewish History in Late Persian and Hellenistic Times," *HTR,* LIX (July, 1966), 201-211.

fifth to the late fourth century, but other like errors can be cited.[73]

TOBIAH

Tobiah appears in Scripture only in connection with the opposition of Sanballat, Tobiah, and Geshem to Nehemiah's work of rebuilding the wall of Jerusalem. ["The sons of Tobiah," who along with others in Zerubbabel's day could not establish their descent (Ezra 2:60; Neh. 7:62), need not concern us here since the evidence for a family relationship to Nehemiah's opponent is lacking.]

Tobiah is denominated "the servant, the Ammonite" (Neh. 2: 10, 19). His activities of opposition parallel those already surveyed for Sanballat (Neh. 4:7) with the exception that his words of ridicule of the wall were: "Yes, what they are building — if a fox goes upon it he will break down their stone wall!" (Neh. 4:3), and he is not included in the proposal that Nehemiah meet them in the plain of Ono (Neh. 6:2 ff.). He is, however, included in the list in the prologue to this episode (Neh. 6:1). He is one of those who hired Shemaiah to attempt to frighten Nehemiah (Neh. 6:10-12) and is included in Nehemiah's imprecation which follows that episode (Neh. 6:14).

Tobiah is the son-in-law of Shecaniah the son of Arah. Nobles of Judah exchanged letters with him and were bound by an oath to him. Tobiah's son had married the daughter of Meshullam, the son of Berechiah. Meshullam was one of the wall builders (cf. Neh. 3:4, 30). Nehemiah accuses the nobles of praising Tobiah to him and of reporting his activities to Tobiah; Tobiah himself wrote letters to make Nehemiah afraid (Neh. 6:17-19).

At a later time, Eliashib, the high priest, had, while Nehemiah was away from Jerusalem prepared a large chamber in the temple for Tobiah. The chamber had previously been used for storage for cereal offerings, frankincense, wine and oil, which were the Levites' portion. Upon his return, Nehemiah threw all the furniture of Tobiah out of the chamber and gave orders

---

73 H. H. Rowley, "Sanballat and the Samaritan Temple," *BJRL,* XXXVIII (Sept., 1955), 166 ff.; "Nehemiah's Mission and its Background," *BJRL,* XXXVII (March, 1955), 528 ff.; J. Stafford Wright, *The Date of Ezra's Coming to Jerusalem* (London: Tyndale Press, 1947), 32 pp.; C. C. Torrey, "Sanballat 'The Horonite,'" *JBL,* XLVII (1928), 384-387; Cowley, *op. cit.,* No. 30; Ralph Marcus, tr. *Josephus* (LCL, VI, Cambridge: Harvard University Press, 1927), 498-511.

that the chamber be cleansed and restored to its prior use (Neh. 13:4-9).

The "Tobiah, servant of the king," met in Lachish Letter No. 3 antedates Nehemiah's opponent by more than a century, and there is no reason to suggest any connection between the two.[74]

A House of Tobiah in Ammon from the Persian period is known and scholars believe Nehemiah's opponent to have been an ancestor of that house. The Tobiah family tomb with the family name inscribed is to be seen at 'Araq el-Emir in Jordan. The inscription has been variously dated from the sixth century B.C. on.[75]

The family name Tobiah is also known to occur in the Zenon papyri which reflect that the name was prominent in Ammon down to Hellenistic times.[76]

Some scholars have also thought Tobiah to have been the ancestor of the house of Tobiah which became a rival of the house of Onias for the high priesthood in Jerusalem.[77]

GESHEM

The third in the trilogy of opponents of Nehemiah is Geshem the Arab. Though not as prominent in the book as the other two, Geshem joins in the ridicule when they hear that the work of building is undertaken. "What is this thing that you are doing? Are you rebelling against the king?" (Neh. 2:19). He joins with Sanballat in inviting Nehemiah to the plain of Ono (Neh. 6:2) and is quoted in Sanballat's letter — the fifth contact with Nehemiah — as saying that Nehemiah and the Jews intended to rebel; that Nehemiah intended to become their king; and that Nehemiah had prophets to proclaim about him, "There is a king in Judah." The letter is a threat to accuse Nehemiah before the king (Neh. 6:6-7).

The Brooklyn Museum has a silver vessel once presented to an Arabic shrine at Tell-el-Maskhūta in the Wadi Tumilat of the eastern part of the Egyptian Delta. The Aramaic inscription on

74 ANET, p. 322.

75 B. Mazar, "The Tobiads," IEJ, VII (1957), 137-145, 229-238; C. C. McCowan, "The 'Araq el-Emir and the Tobiads," BA, XX (Sept. 1957), 63-76; Josephus Ant. xii. 4. 11 (228-233); W. F. Albright, The Archaeology of Palestine (Baltimore: Penguin Books, 1951), p. 149.

76 C. C. Edgar, "Selected Papyri from the archives of Zenon," Annales du service des antiquités de l'Égypte, XVII (1918), 164-166, 231-232; H. Willrich, "Zur Geschichte der Tobiaden," Archiv für papyrus Förschung, VII (1924), 61-64.

77 II Macc. 3:11; Josephus Ant. xii. 4. 1 ff. (158).

the vessel is to be dated to the end of the fifth century B.C. and states that the vessel was presented by "Cain (Qainu) son of Geshem (Gashmu), king of Qedar."[78]

Geshem is also known from a Lihyanite inscription where he is associated with the Persian governor Dedan.[79] As translated by Winnett, the inscription reads: "Niran the son of Hadiru inscribed his name in the days of Jashm the son of Shahar and ᶜAbd the governor of Dedan. . . ."

TATTENAI

Tattenai is the governor of the province, Beyond the River, during the reign of Darius, who, along with Shetharbozenai and their associates, challenged the right of Zerubbabel and Jeshua to build the temple (Ezra 5:3). They proceeded to write a letter to Darius informing him of the project and cautioning of alleged dangers to the king should the project be completed (Ezra 5:6 ff.). They in turn received an order to allow the work to proceed (Ezra 6:6) with which order they complied (Ezra 6:13).

Pointing out the unacceptability of an earlier proposed identification of Tattenai with Ushtani, a figure known from Babylonian tablets, it has been argued that there is a cuneiform occurrence of Tattenai's name in a Babylonian document dated 502 B.C. and published by Ungnad in 1907. The passage refers to a slave of "Ta-ta-tan-ni, governor (*pahat*) of Ebir-nari."[80]

JEHOHANAN, SON OF ELIASHIB

Ezra, following his learning of the mixed marriages in the post-exilic Jewish community, went into the chamber of Jehohanan, the son of Eliashib, where he spent the night in fasting

---

78 Isaac Rabinowitz, "Aramaic Inscriptions of the Fifth Century B.C.E. from a North-Arab Shrine in Egypt," *JNES*, XV (January, 1956), 1-9; F. M. Cross, Jr., "Geshem the Arabian, Enemy of Nehemiah," *BA*, XVII (1955), 46-47.

79 Rabinowitz, *op. cit.*, p. 6, n. 39; F. V. Winnett, *A Study of the Lihyanite and Thamudic Inscriptions* (1937), pp. 14-16, 50-51; H. Grimme, "Beziehungen zwischen dem Staate der Lihjän und dem Achämenidenreiche," *Orientalische Literaturzeitung*, XLIV (1941), 343; A. J. Jaussen and R. Savignac, *Mission archéologique en Arabie* (Paris: Librairie Paul Geuthner, (1914), No. 349.

80 *Op. cit.*, pp. 240-244; A. T. Olmstead, "Tattenai, Governor of 'Across the River,'" *JNES*, III (1944), 46; W. Eilers, *Iranische Beamtennamen in der keilinschriftlischen Überliferung* (Leipzig: Deutsche morgenländische Gesellschaft, 1940), pp. 35-37.

(Ezra 10:6; cf. I Esdras 9:1). Following an assembly of the people, Ezra received a pledge that the marriages would be dissolved. Eliashib was high priest during the days of Nehemiah (Neh. 3:1; 13:4) and is said to have had a grandson named Jonathan: Eliashib was the father of Joiada, Joiada the father of Jonathan, and Jonathan the father of Juddua (Neh. 12:10-11).[81] The last figure in this genealogy is placed by Josephus in the time of Alexander the Great.[82] Long ago Albright attempted to solve the problem by arguing that Josephus' figure is a different Jaddua from the Biblical figure.[83]

The petition from Yedoniah in Elephantine, dated 407 B.C., addressed to Bigvai, governor of Judea, states that a letter had previously been sent to Johanan the high priest and his colleagues, the priests, in Jerusalem.[84]

Jonathan is not said specifically to be High Priest in Ezra and in Nehemiah, and the relationship of Jonathan to the problem of the order of appearances of Ezra-Nehemiah is one of the acute problems of Biblical study. Nevertheless, despite the fact that Jehohanan is a common name, both sides of the debate generally assume that Jehohanan of the papyrus and Jehohanan, son of Eliashib, are to be identified with each other.[85]

SUMMARY

The Persian period of Biblical history brings before us four kings of Persia: Cyrus, Darius, Ahasuerus, and Artaxerxes concerning all of whom there is clear historical material. In addition to these Persians, on a lesser rank, there is Tattenai, governor of Beyond the River. The period presents us with two Israelite figures: Mordecai and Jehohanan, son of Eliashib, with the identification of the latter on a more solid basis than that of the former. There are three non-Israelite Palestinians: Sanballat, Tobiah, and Geshem, who seem well enough established.

This period furnishes at least nine recognized, indisputable figures and one additional suggested figure (Mordecai) who has not yet gained general acceptance. The person of Darius the Mede remains an unknown figure outside of the Biblical narratives about him.

---

81 Cf. v. 22 and Josephus *Ant*. xi. 7. 1 (297).
82 *Ant*. xi. 7. 4 (321 ff.).
83 "The Date and Personality of the Chronicler," *JBL*, XL (1921), 112, 122.
84 Cowley, *op. cit*., No. 30, 1. 18; *ANET*, p. 492.
85 But see Heinisch, *op. cit*., p. 331.

VII

IN THE FULLNESS OF TIME

The main actors of the New Testament drama are hardly known outside of it and its sphere of influence. However, the New Testament story occurred at a definite time and place in history, and at least one New Testament writer, Luke, was interested in making synchronisms between Gospel events and events in the wider Roman world of the time. These synchronisms add immensely to our list of names of known historical figures who came into contact in some way with major or minor characters of the Biblical drama.

The New Testament history spans something less than three quarters of one century excluding events alluded to in the book of Revelation. With Christianity arising as it did in the full light of history, literary sources furnish far more illustrative materials than does archaeology itself. For the Old Testament the opposite was true. Since, however, information on Bible characters from any source is welcomed by Biblical students, it seems wise in this section to call attention to the material from both types of sources with some indication of the value of each. We shall begin with John the Baptist, Jesus, and James, and then turn to Roman officials, next to the Herod family, and finally to figures of less renown.

GOSPEL PERSONNEL

John the Baptist

The birth of John, the forerunner of the Christian movement, is related only in Luke, but the work of John is surveyed in each of the four Gospels and is also alluded to in the book of Acts (Acts 1:5; 11:16; 18:25; 19:1-5). The death of John at the hands

of Herod is related in each of the synoptic gospels (Mark 6:
14 ff.; Matt. 14:3-12; Luke 3:19-20).

John has entered heavily into recent study of possible contacts between early Christianity and the Qumran community
which preserved for us the Dead Sea scrolls. Numerous recent
studies dealing with John and his movement have appeared.[1]
However, the possible contacts of John with Qumran literature
are theological rather than personal. Archaeologists have found
nothing directly connected with John.

Josephus has an account of the death of John which he relates
in connection with a defeat administered to Herod Antipas by
Aretas IV whose daughter Herod had abandoned in order to
marry Herodias. The passage reads:

> But to some of the Jews the destruction of Herod's army
> seemed to be divine vengeance, for his treatment of John, sur-
> named the Baptist. For Herod had put him to death, though
> he was a good man and had exhorted the Jews to lead righteous
> lives, to practice justice towards their fellows and piety towards
> God, and so doing to join in baptism. In his view this was a
> necessary preliminary if baptism was to be acceptable to God.
> They must not employ it to gain pardon for whatever sins they
> had committed, but as a consecration of the body implying
> that the soul was already thoroughly cleansed by right be-
> haviour. When others too joined the crowds about him, be-
> cause they were aroused to the highest degree by his sermons,
> Herod became alarmed. Eloquence that had so great effect on
> mankind might lead to some form of sedition, for it looked as
> if they would be guided by John in everything that they did.
> Herod decided therefore that it would be much better to strike
> first and be rid of him before his work led to an uprising, than
> to wait for an upheaval, get involved in a difficult situation
> and see his mistake. Though John, because of Herod's suspi-
> cions, was brought in chains to Machaerus, the stronghold that
> we have previously mentioned, and there put to death, yet the
> verdict of the Jews was that the destruction visited upon
> Herod's army was a vindication of John, since God saw fit to
> inflict such a blow on Herod.[2]

---

1 J. Danielou, *The Work of John the Baptist*, trans. by Joseph Horn
(Baltimore: Helicon, 1966), 148 pp.; C. H. Kraeling, *John the Baptist*
(New York: Scribner's Sons, 1951), 218 pp.; C. H. H. Scobie, *John the
Baptist* (Philadelphia: Fortress Press, 1964), 224 pp.; Jean Steinmann,
Saint John the Baptist and the Desert Tradition, trans. by M. Boyes (London: Longmans Green and Co., 1958), 191 pp.; W. Wink, *John the Baptist in the Gospel Tradition* (London: Cambridge University Press, 1968),
131 pp.
2 *Ant.* xviii. 5. 2 (116-119).

The passage is usually thought to be authentic, but the contrasts between this story and the Gospel materials are obvious. Josephus gives an entirely different significance to John's baptism from that "for the remission of sins" found in the Gospels (Mark 1:4). John's denunciation of Herod's marriage is here passed over in silence. On the other hand, Josephus supplies a political motif for Herod's action which is not suggested in the Gospels. He also supplies a place of imprisonment — Machaerus — not found in the Gospels.

Jesus

Outside of the Gospels Jesus attracted no attention of writers who are strictly his contemporaries. In fact, there is a sparsity of written material for this whole period. Some years later at the beginning of the second century, scattered notices begin to emerge. The earliest pagan to allude to Jesus seems to be Pliny who, about A.D. 110, wrote from Bithynia to Emperor Trajan requesting instructions about how to deal with Christians in his district. He regarded Christianity as a base and degrading superstition. He tells of some who when called upon "reviled Christ," but he also speaks of a Christian meeting in which before dawn they sing a hymn to Christ as God. Trajan commends Pliny's procedures, but says that Christians are not to be sought out.[3] Shortly after Pliny, Tacitus, about A.D. 115 in describing Nero's persecutions, a half century before, reported that the name Christian was derived from Christ, "who had been put to death in the reign of Tiberius by the procurator Pontius Pilate."[4] Only a few years later Suetonius reported that Claudius in a year equivalent to A.D. 49/50 drove the Jews out of Rome because of riots at the instigation of *Chrestus*.[5] It has been widely assumed that this was a Jewish-Christian quarrel and, if this is true, it would be the earliest date to which secular evidence for the movement can be traced.

The statements found in the text of Josephus about Jesus, though usually accepted as authentic until the rise of the critical movement, have been under heavy challenge since that time. Both E. Schürer[6] and J. Juster[7] insisted that the material

---

3 Pliny *Epistle* x. 96, 97.
4 *Annals* xv. 44.
5 *Claudius* 25. 4.
6 *A History of the Jewish People in the time of Jesus Christ,* trans. by John MacPherson (Edinburgh: T. & T. Clark, 1898), I, 2. 143-149.
7 *Les Juifs dans l'empire Romain* (New York: Burt Franklin, reprinted from 1914), I, 13, n. 4.

is a Christian interpolation. H. St. John Thackeray, a generation ago, analyzed the style of the passages and concluded that they were authentic,[8] but Thackeray has by no means convinced all. R. Eisler failed to convince scholars with his system of identifying the degree of interpolation,[9] but the editor of the Loeb edition of Josephus remarks: "The most probable view seems to be that our text represents substantially what Josephus wrote but that some alterations have been made by a Christian interpolator."[10]

The first of the passages is that in which Josephus discusses James. Josephus describes him as "the brother of Jesus who was called Christ."[11] This phrase is quoted by Origen in his Commentary on Matthew about A.D. 230.[12]

It is, however, the second passage which is most debatable. It was not quoted by Origen, but was quoted by Eusebius in A.D. 324[13] and then somewhat later by Jerome.[14]

> About this time there lived Jesus, a wise man, if indeed one ought to call him a man. For he was one who wrought surprising feats and was a teacher of such people as accept the truth gladly. He won over many Jews and many of the Greeks. He was the Messiah. When Pilate, upon hearing him accused by men of the highest standing amongst us, had condemned him to be crucified, those who had in the first place come to love him did not give up their affection for him. On the third day he appeared to them restored to life, for the prophets of God had prophesied these things and countless other marvellous things about him. And the tribe of the Christians, so called after him, has still to this day not disappeared.[15]

The passage is found in all manuscripts of Josephus. Large in the controversy over the authenticity of the passage is the fact that Origen explicitly states that Josephus did not believe that

---

8 *Josephus, The Man and the Historian* (New York: Jewish Institute of Religion Press, 1929), pp. 124-153. For a statement of the converse case, see S. Zeitlin, *The Rise and Fall of the Judaean State* (Philadelphia: Jewish Publication Society, 1967), II, 373-378.

9 *The Messiah Jesus,* trans. by A. H. Krappe (London: Methuen, 1931), pp. 49 ff.

10 L. H. Feldman, *Josephus* (LCL; Cambridge: Harvard University Press, 1965), Vol. IX, 49, n. b.

11 *Ant.* xx. 9. 1 (197-203).

12 X. 17 (*G.C.S.* 40, 22); cf. *Contra Celsum* i. 47.

13 *H.E.* i. 11. 7 ff.; *Dem. Evang.* iii. 5. 105 (*G.C.S.* 23, 130).

14 *De Vir. Ill.* 12 (*P.L.* 23, 642).

15 Josephus *Ant.* xviii. 3. 3 (63-64).

Jesus was the Christ.[16] There is also the logical question of whether Josephus, a loyal Pharisee, would have written the phrase "He was the Messiah." The Slavonic edition of Josephus has yet additional sections that are usually questioned.

No authentic relics of Jesus have survived. Even the identification of the exact places of his birth and burial are involved in conjecture with several centuries lapsing between the time the events occurred and the time the identifications were made.

James

The lists of brothers of Jesus include the name of James (Mark 6:3; Matt. 13:55) to whom Jesus appeared after his resurrection (I Cor. 15:7). James became a leader in the church in Jerusalem. At the gathering concerned with the keeping of the Law, it was he who summarized the meeting and proposed a program for the Gentiles (Acts 15:13-21). Those opponents of Paul who came to Antioch claimed to be from James (Gal. 2:12). In the presence of James and the elders Paul rehearsed his ministry among the Gentiles at the end of his third missionary journey (Acts 21:18 ff.). It is doubtless he who is alluded to in the opening of the Epistle of James as "a servant of God and of the Lord Jesus Christ" (James 1:1).

Josephus reports the death of James which occurred during a period of turmoil between the terms of office of two of the procurators, Festus and Albinus:

> Possessed of such a character, Ananus thought that he had a favourable opportunity because Festus was dead and Albinus was still on the way. And so he convened the judges of the Sanhedrin and brought before them a man called James, the brother of Jesus who was called the Christ, and certain others. He accused them of having transgressed the law and delivered them up to be stoned.[17]

Unlike the testimony about Jesus, this passage about James is usually thought to be authentic. A Christian writer of the second century, Hegesippus, says that James was thrown down from the "pinnacle" of the temple, stoned, and finally killed by a fuller's club.[18]

---

16 C. Celsum i. 47; Comm. in Matt. X. 17 (G.C.S. 40, 22).
17 Ant. xx. 9. 1 (200).
18 Cited in Eusebius H.E. ii. 23. 3 ff.

ROMAN OFFICIALS

A. *The Caesars*

Of New Testament writers only Luke refers to Roman imperial figures. Emperors Augustus (Luke 2:1) and Tiberius (Luke 3:1) are each alluded to once by name in the Gospel. In the Acts Claudius is met by name twice (Acts 11:28; 18:2) and is the only emperor so frequently mentioned. It is also likely that he is alluded to in Acts 17:7 when the men of Thessalonica accuse Paul and his companions of transgressing the decrees of Caesar. Nero is merely called Caesar (Acts 25:8, 11, 12, 21; 26:32; 27:24), Sebastos (Acts 25:21, 25), and lord (Acts 25:26), but is not called by his personal name.[19]

19. AUGUSTUS CAESAR, ruler of the Roman Empire at the time of the birth of Jesus. Courtesy, Museo Nazionale, Naples

20. THE ROMAN EMPEROR TIBERIU Courtesy, Museo Nazionale, Naples

Augustus Caesar

The birth of Jesus is dated in Luke's account by a census of Augustus: "In those days there went out a decree of Caesar Augustus that all the world should be enrolled" (Luke 2:1).

19 H. J. Cadbury, *The Book of Acts in History* (London: A. & C. Black, 1955), p. 58.

While there is ample material on Augustus himself, who exercised emperorship from 27 B.C. to A.D. 14, no other record of his decree for a census covering the world (*oikumene*) has been preserved. This matter has been and continues to be one of the most debated topics of gospel study.

Following the battle of Actium in 31 B.C. in which he defeated the forces of Antony and Cleopatra, Augustus came to have dominion over Palestine. Remnants of his rule in Palestine include remains of temples built in his honor at Caesarea and at Samaria by Herod the Great. His decrees in favor of the Jews have been preserved by Josephus.[20] Some coins carry his image and name. Such a coin issued by Philip the Tetrarch and dated year 5 (i.e., A.D. 1-2) is inscribed: "For Sebastos (i.e., Augustus) Caesar."[21]

Tiberius Caesar

Tiberius appears in the New Testament only in Luke's synchronism, which dates the beginning of the ministry of John the Baptist:

> In the fifteenth year of the reign of Tiberius Caesar . . . the word of God came to John the son of Zechariah in the wilderness (Luke 3:1, 2).

However, references in the Gospel to Caesar in episodes such as the matter of the inscription on tribute money (Matt. 22:17-21; Mark 12:14-17; Luke 20:22-25; 23:2) and the cry "You are not Caesar's friend" (John 19:12-15) also refer to him.

In 4 B.C., Tiberius had been adopted by Augustus as his heir. Following the death of Augustus, the senate named Tiberius emperor on September 17, A.D. 14. During his reign, some Jewish problems arose in Rome which called forth regulatory decrees. Tiberius died on Capri on March 16, A.D. 37.

The death of Jesus under Tiberius is alluded to by Tacitus,[22] though this testimony need not be independent of Jewish and Christian tradition. Remnants of his rule in Palestine are to be seen in the examples of the denarius with his portrait and the inscription: "Tiberius Caesar, son of the deified Augustus, Augustus." Philip is the first Jewish ruler in Palestine to use the effigy

---

20 *Ant.* xvi. 6. 2 (162-167).
21 A. Reifenberg, *Israel's History in Coins* (London: East and West Library, 1953), p. 24, No. 8.
22 *Annals*, xv. 44.

of the Roman emperor on his coins.[23] Other examples of coins issued by his procurators are cited in A. Kindler's study.[24] Also, a stone was found in 1961 in the theater in Caesarea which, in addition to bearing the name of Pontius Pilate, honors the name of Tiberius. It has been conjectured that the stone was originally a dedicatory formula of some important building in Tiberius' honor.[25]

Claudius Caesar

Claudius is met by name twice in the New Testament and as previously noted, is the only emperor so frequently mentioned. It is also likely that he is alluded to in Acts 17:7 when the men of Thessalonica accuse Paul and his companions of transgressing the decrees of Caesar. A great famine broke out in Judea in Claudius' reign (Acts 11:28), and at a later date he "commanded all Jews to leave Rome" (Acts 18:2). This last event is cited to explain the migration of Aquila and Priscilla from Rome to Corinth.

There is no scarcity of material on Claudius (who reigned from A.D. 41-54) in classical sources. Conditions of the Jews under Claudius are set forth by Josephus where certain pro-Jewish edicts are cited[26] and in certain papyrus finds such as the letter which he sent to the people of Alexandria dealing with friction between the Jewish and Greek population.[27] Christianity had just begun its spread at the beginning of his reign, but by its end had spread through Galatia, Macedonia, and Achaia, and at the time of his death Paul was at work in Ephesus.[28]

Of particular interest for our present purposes is the fact that Suetonius informs us of a series of droughts during Tiberius' reign.[29] Josephus tells of charity in the years A.D. 44-48 by Queen Helena, who purchased and imported grain and figs to

---

23 A. Reifenberg, *Ancient Jewish Coins* (Jerusalem: Rubin Mass, 4th ed., 1965), p. 19, No. 43.

24 "More Dates on the Coins of the Procurators," *IEJ*, VI (1956), 54-57.

25 Jerry Vardaman, "A New Inscription which Mentions Pilate as 'Prefect,'" *JBL*, LXXXI (1962), 70-71.

26 *Ant.* xix. 5. 1 ff. (274 ff.).

27 H. I. Bell, *Jews and Christians in Egypt* (London: British Museum, 1924), pp. 1 ff.

28 F. F. Bruce, "Christianity under Claudius," *BJRL*, XLIV (1962), 321.

29 *Claudius* 18. 2.

distribute to the distressed of Jerusalem.[30] It is likely that this is the famine to which allusion is made in the book of Acts.[31]

Claudius' action against the Jews in Rome is reported by Suetonius, who wrote *ca.* A.D. 120:

> Since the Jews constantly made disturbances at the instigation of Chrestus, he expelled them from Rome.[32]

The decree is discussed more fully by a later writer, Dio Cassius, who states that the decree forbade assemblies:

> As for the Jews who had again increased so greatly that by reason of this multitude it would have been hard without raising a tumult to bar them from the city, he did not drive them out, but ordered them, while continuing their traditional mode of life, not to hold meetings.[33]

Yet still a third writer Orosius (fifth century), who claims to derive his information from Josephus, dates the edict in Claudius' ninth year (A.D. 49-50).[34]

Coins issued by Felix have the name of Claudius inscribed on them.[35]

Nero

Nero is not called by his personal name in the New Testament, but is alluded to repeatedly in the last part of Acts under the name Caesar (Acts 25:8, 11, 12, 21; 26:32; 27:24) and by the titles, "Sebastos" (Acts 25:21, 25) and "lord" (Acts 25:26). Paul's appeal to Caesar was an appeal to Nero and it was to Nero that he was sent by Festus.

Vicissitudes of the Jewish people under Nero's rule (A.D. 54-68) are surveyed by Josephus.[36] His rule in Palestine is further represented by coins carrying the likeness of his head and his name.[37] Nero's persecution of Christians following the fire in Rome, July 19, A.D. 64, is surveyed by Tacitus.[38]

---

30 *Ant.* xx. 2. 5 (49-53).
31 Bruce, *op. cit.*, p. 309.
32 *Claudius* 25. 4.
33 *Roman History* lx. 6. 6.
34 *Historiarum adversum Paganos* vii. 6, 15 (*C.S.E.L.* V, 451).
35 Ya°akov Meshorer, *Jewish Coins of the Second Temple Period*, trans. by I. H. Levine (Tel-Aviv: Am Hassefer, 1967), p. 174.
36 *War* ii. 13. 1 ff. (250 ff.); *Ant.* xx. 8. 1 ff. (150 ff.), 9 (182 ff.), *et passim.*
37 Reifenberg, *Ancient Jewish Coins*, p. 49, Nos. 78 & 79.
38 *Annals* xv. 44.

21. NERO, persecutor of the church. Courtesy, N. Stournaras

B. *Provincial Officials*

Quirinius

Luke dates the birth of Jesus from a census made at the decree of Augustus during the governorship of Quirinius. "This was the first enrollment, when Quirinius was the governor of Syria" (2:2). From information given in the previous chapter (1:5) it must be deduced that this census was taken while Herod was reigning in Judea.

P. Sulpicius Quirinius and his census are among the most debated questions in New Testament study. Josephus tells of a census by Quirinius, governor of Syria, when Coponius was governor of Judea which led to the uprising of Judas of Galilee.[39] This census would date A.D. 6-7 and is perhaps alluded to by Gamaliel in Acts (5:37). It followed, according to Josephus, the deposing of Archelaus when Palestine for the first time came under direct Roman government.[40] This would, of course, be too late to be the census spoken of in Luke.

This census in the time of Coponius is a provincial census (*apographe*) hardly to be described by the term, "whole world (*oikumene*)," and dates about ten years too late for a census taken in the time of Herod. In addition to the problems of date and extent, the census question demands an interpretation of the phrase, "the first census when Quirinius was governor of Syria," and the question of whether "governor (*hegemon*)" is a proper title for the position Quirinius held in the time of Herod.

Ramsay argued on the basis of evidence from an inscription he found at Antioch in Pisidia that Quirinius held office in Syria as *legatus* (prior to the census under Coponius) either in 11 or 10 to 8 or 7 B.C.[41] The inscription describes him as *Duumvir* (honorary mayor) of Antioch. It is, of course, strange that Josephus has no record of a census at this earlier date, and though he does not actually say that it is the first, he treats the later one as an innovation. The question continues to be a debated one.

Lysanias

The appearance of John the Baptist is synchronized with the fifteenth year (A.D. 29) of the reign of Tiberius Caesar and with officials within the Palestinian area. One of these is Lysanias, "tetrarch of Abilene" (Luke 3:1).

At one time this Lysanias was indeed a problematic figure. An earlier Lysanias, who occupied the throne of Chalcis, who was executed by Mark Antony at the instigation of Cleopatra in 36 B.C., was known to Josephus[42] and to Dio Cassius.[43] This figure is, of course, too early to have been active when John the Baptist began his ministry.

---

39 *Ant.* xvii. 13. 5 (355); xviii. 1. 1 (2).

40 *War* ii. 8. 1 (118); vii. 8. 1 (253).

41 W. M. Ramsay, *The Bearing of Recent Discovery on the Trustworthiness of the New Testament* (Grand Rapids: Baker Book House, 1953, reprint of 1911 edition), pp. 275 ff.

42 *Ant.* xv. 4. 1 (92).

43 *Roman History* xlix. 32. 5.

Already from Josephus, however, some passages may indicate a second Lysanias. When in A.D. 53 Claudius enlarged the territory of Agrippa II, Josephus includes in the areas: "Lysanias' former tetrarchy of Abila."[44] Elsewhere in dealing with the same topic he says, "But he also added Abila, which had been ruled by Lysanias."[45] And again he speaks of "a further principality known as the kingdom of Lysanias."[46] While it is not impossible that they could refer to the figure slain by Mark Antony, it has been argued by Creed and others that they are better explained if a second Lysanias is postulated.[47]

It is also likely that two Greek inscriptions refer to this second Lysanias. The first speaks of a Lysanias with Zenodorus son of Lysanias the tetrarch.[48] The second, found at Abila, cannot be dated earlier than the time of Tiberius, is a dedication of a temple, and reads:

> . . . for the salvation of the Lord's Imperial and their whole household, by Nymphaeus a freedman of Lysanias the tetrarch.[49]

Pontius Pilate

Following the removal of Archaelaus from his office in A.D. 6, Judea was made into a Roman province under procurators appointed by the senate. The seat of government was shifted to Caesarea. Of the procurators only Pontius Pilate, who is number five in the sequence, appears in the New Testament. Pilate is mentioned fifty-three times.

At the beginning of the gospel story the appearance of John the Baptist is dated by the governorship in Judea of Pontius Pilate (Luke 3:1). Later, when Jesus was reminded of certain Galileans whose blood Pilate had mingled with their sacrifices, he used the episode as an occasion to issue a call to repentance (Luke 13:1).

Pilate is forever remembered in infamy for his role in the condemnation of Jesus, which role is first mentioned in each of the Gospels, but is also recalled in the sermons of Acts (3:13;

---

44 *Ant.* xx. 7. 1 (138).
45 *Ibid.*, xix. 5. 1 (275).
46 Josephus *War* ii. 11. 5 (215).
47 J. M. Creed, *The Gospel According to Luke* (London: Macmillan, 1953), pp. 307-309.
48 *C.I.G.*, III, 4523.
49 *Ibid.*, 4521; R. K. Harrison, *Archaeology of the New Testament* (London: The English Universities Press, 1964), p. 27.

4:27; 13:28). The first Epistle to Timothy also refers to the trial before Pilate (6:13).

Jesus was delivered to Pilate by the Jewish officials after a preliminary hearing before Caiaphas (Matt. 27:2; Mark 15:1). The silence of Jesus to his various questions caused Pilate to marvel (Mark 15:5; Matt. 27:14). It was he who sent Jesus to Herod (Luke 23:12); who came out of the Judgment Hall to the pavement as a concession to the Jews (John 18:28 ff.); who scourged Jesus (John 19:1 ff.); and who offered the Jews the choice of Jesus or Barabbas (Matt. 27:17 ff.). Despite his repeated insistence that he found Jesus innocent (in Luke this assertion is made three times), he handed him over. It was he who washed his hands when he could not dissuade the Jews (Matt. 27:24); who composed the inscription of the cross; and who refused later to change it (John 19:19-22). From Pilate, Joseph of Arimathea sought the body of Jesus for burial (Mark 15:43; Luke 23:52; John 19:38), and from him, the Pharisees sought permission to station a guard at the tomb (Matt. 27:62-66).

Some events of the career of Pilate, A.D. 26-36, are traced out by Josephus[50] without allusion to the Gospel episodes. These include conflict over taking Roman standards with the Emperor's image into Jerusalem and conflict over using temple funds for construction of an aqueduct. A conflict over gilded votive shields is also related by Philo.[51] Pilate was ordered by the Emperor to remove them. The roughshod way in which Pilate trampled upon the feelings of the Jewish people in these episodes shows clearly that Pilate was not always conciliatory toward the Jewish people. Philo accuses him of being guilty of rape, insolence, murder, and inhumanity and describes him as a person of "inflexible, stubborn, and cruel disposition." Yet another conflict involved brutally dispersing Samaritans from Mt. Gerizim. As a result of a complaint over this incident Pilate was recalled to Rome.[52]

Tacitus, who wrote *ca.* A.D. 115, in connection with a description of acts of Nero, speaks of the execution of Jesus by Pontius Pilate in the reign of Tiberius:

> Therefore to scotch the rumor, Nero substituted as culprits, and punished with the utmost refinements of cruelty, a class of men, loathed for their vices, whom the crowd styled Christians. Christus, the founder of the name, had undergone the

50 *Ant.* xviii. 3. 1 (55 ff.); *War* ii. 9. 2 (169 ff.).
51 *Leg. ad Caium* 38 (299).
52 Josephus *Ant.* xviii. 4. 2 (88 ff.).

death penalty in the reign of Tiberius, by the sentence of the procurator Pontius Pilate.[53]

Since it is entirely possible that Tacitus derived his information from Christian tradition, he cannot be claimed with assurance as an independent witness.

In 1961 in excavations in Caesarea a reused stone from the theater was discovered bearing the name of Pontius Pilate. This Latin inscription, the first to be found for this procurator,[54] is now in the Israel Museum in Jerusalem.[55] Previously Pilate was known only from the Gospels, from the writings of Josephus, Philo, and Tacitus, and from later apocryphal materials. The Latin inscription of the stone is defective, but in translation perhaps reads: "Tiberium [? of the Caesareans?] Pontius Pilate, Prefect of Judea [. . . ? has given?]." The New Testament calls Pilate "governor (*hegemon*)," which might be used for any official; the new inscription calls him "prefect"; whereas, both Josephus and Tacitus call him a "procurator."

Heathen symbols were used on coins struck during Pilate's term of office and are unique examples of such symbols for the period of the procurators.[56]

Felix

After the period of the first group of procurators, for a brief interlude of three years (A.D. 41-44) Judea was ruled by Herod Agrippa I, and was then again returned to the rule of a second group of procurators. Of these Felix and Festus appear in the New Testament.

Following Paul's arrest in Jerusalem, he was sent to Caesarea to Felix to safeguard him from danger from the mob which had sworn to take his life (Acts 23:24). Along with Paul, the chief captain, Claudius Lysias, sent a letter to Felix explaining the problem (Acts 23:26). Before Felix, Paul answered the charges brought by the orator Tertullus, but Felix delayed a verdict. Felix, with his wife Drusilla, heard Paul on other occasions with additional delays. On one of these occasions Paul "reasoned of righteousness, self-control and of judgment to come" (Acts 24:25). For two years Felix kept Paul in prison. The writer of Acts suggests he hoped to receive a bribe. Eventually when he

---

53 *Annals* xv. 44.
54 Vardaman, *op. cit.*, pp. 70-71.
55 *Provisional Guide* (Jerusalem: Israel Museum, 1965), No. 169.
56 Baruch Kanael, "Ancient Jewish Coins and Their Historical Importance," *BA*, XXVI (1963), 54-55.

was succeeded by Festus, Felix left Paul in prison to please the Jews (Acts 24:27).

The career of Felix (A.D. 52-60), whose full name is Antonius Felix, may be traced through data furnished by Josephus, Tacitus, and Suetonius. His name also occurs in a Latin inscription.[57] These relate the story of his rise to power, some of the vicissitudes of his term of office, and the circumstances under which he was replaced by Festus, but they give us nothing of his relationship to the Apostle.

Felix, the brother of an influential Roman named Pallas,[58] was a freedman and is reported to have been a favorite of Claudius.[59] Once appointed procurator, he put down uprisings by "robbers and imposters,"[60] but was not beyond using their services at times for his own ends such as that of the murder of the high priest Jonathan.[61] Felix persuaded Drusilla to leave her husband Azizus, king of Emesa, and to Felix she bore a son, Agrippa.[62] She was only one of his three royal wives.[63] Although Tacitus ascribes to him procuratorship of Judea while Cumanus was procurator of Galilee,[64] historians are more inclined to follow Josephus, who has him succeed Cumanus in Judea.[65]

The Romans were not at all complimentary to Felix. Tacitus reports that he believed he could commit all kinds of evil with inpunity[66] and that he, "indulging in every kind of barbarity and lust, exercised the power of a king in the spirit of a slave."[67]

Felix was recalled over his handling of a disturbance in Caesarea. Despite the accusation of his opponents, he escaped punishment through the intervention of his brother Pallas.[68]

Porcius Festus

Festus succeeded Felix as procurator of Judea (Acts 24:27). Upon his coming to his province he visited Jerusalem where

---

57 C.I.L., V. 34.
58 Josephus Ant. xx. 7. 1 (137).
59 Suetonius Claudius 28.
60 Josephus War ii. 13. 2-3 (252 ff.).
61 Josephus Ant. xx. 8. 5 (162 f.).
62 Ibid., xx. 7. 2 (141 ff.).
63 Suetonius Claudius 28.
64 Annals xii. 54.
65 Ant. xx. 6. 3-7. 1 (134 ff.); War ii. 12. 8 (247 ff.); see note in Loeb edition, IX, 461, n. e.
66 Annals xii. 54.
67 Tacitus History v. 9.
68 Josephus Ant. xx. 8. 9 (182).

Paul's accusers urged that he send Paul to Jerusalem for trial. Festus countered by proposing that they send accusers to Caesarea to which he was going shortly (Acts 25:1-5). At a hearing before Festus, Paul was given an option of going to Jerusalem to be tried and answered by appealing to Caesar. Before Festus had opportunity to send Paul to Rome, King Agrippa visited Caesarea, and Festus, confessing that he was ignorant of what specific charges should be made against Paul, brought the matter to Agrippa's attention. The quarrel seemed to Festus to be over the Jews' superstition and about a certain dead Jesus whom Paul alleged to be alive (Acts 25:13-27). In the course of the hearing, Festus accused Paul of being mad because of his great learning, which charge Paul denied (Acts 26:24-25). Agrippa suggested to Festus that Paul could have been freed had he not made his appeal (Acts 26:32).

Outside of Acts, the procuratorship of Festus (A.D. 60-62) is surveyed only by Josephus. Josephus has nothing to say about Festus' relation to Paul. As valuable as the specific date of Festus' entrance into his office would be for establishing the chronology of this part of Paul's career, it is a debated question with opinions varying from A.D. 55 to 60.

Festus proved helpless to stop the conflicts between Jews and Pagans that had begun prior to his term of office in Caesarea. He struggled to regulate the Sicarii, whom he regarded as bandits, and a number were executed. He sided with Agrippa II in a quarrel with the priests over a wall that would block Agrippa's view of activities in the temple. The case was appealed to Rome. Festus died in office before a decision was rendered, but the wall was left standing.[69]

Sergius Paulus

Paul's first missionary journey brought him to Paphos where he found "the proconsul, Sergius Paulus, a man of intelligence" in the power of a Jewish false prophet named Bar-Jesus. After a clash with Bar-Jesus (Elymas), Paul was able to lead the proconsul to belief (Acts 13:6-12).

It is known that Cyprus was a senatorial province ruled over by a proconsul from the time of Augustus.[70] Some scholars, such as Lightfoot, have attempted to find evidence for Sergius Paulus in the inscription discovered at Soli, Cyprus, which re-

69 *Ibid.*, xx. 8. 9-11 (182 ff.).
70 Cadbury, *op. cit.*, p. 42.

fers to a Proconsul Paulus. Additional study has shown, however, the impossibility of dating the Paulus concerned to the
time of Paul's visit. T. Mommsen argued that the Paulus of the
inscription was Paulus Fabius Maximus, who was proconsul in
11 B.C.[71] Also now refuted is Lightfoot's effort to identify Sergius Paulus with a figure mentioned by the historian Pliny as
one of his sources for his *Naturalis Historia,* book ii. Additional
study of the manuscripts supports the reading in this passage of
Sergius Plautus rather than Sergius Paulus.[72]

There is, however, a Latin inscription which in a list of names
of curators of the Tiber includes the name of one L. Sergius
Paulus.[73] If Sergius Paulus went immediately after his curator-
ship of the Tiber to Cyprus as proconsul, the date would cor-
respond with that of the account given in Acts.[74] The inscription does not connect him with Cyprus or with the Apostle Paul.
Ramsay made other conjectural identifications from inscriptions
in other areas,[75] but these are not now generally accepted.

Gallio

Jews of Corinth brought a complaint against Paul before Gallio, proconsul of Achaia, charging: "This man is persuading
men to worship God contrary to the law." When Paul was about
to defend himself, Gallio, while ready to hear criminal charges,
refused to hear the case because of its dealing with "questions
about words and names and Jewish law" and drove them from
the tribunal. Gallio also closed his eyes to the beating administered Sosthenes in front of the tribunal (Acts 18:12-17).

Gallio, the older brother of the philosopher Seneca, was born
Marcus Annaeus Novatus, but was adopted by a rich man,
Lucius Junius Gallio, by which procedure his full name came
to be Lucius Junius Gallio Annaeus. The story of his career can
be traced through allusions from a number of classical writers.

Most important of all, however, is a Greek inscription known
from four fragments of a limestone tablet which were found at
Delphi in 1905. The tablet is thought to be a letter from the
Emperor Claudius to the people of Delphi which from its allusion to the Emperor's twenty-sixth acclamation suggests a date

---

71 "Die Rechtsverhältnisse des Apostls Paulus," ZNTW, II (1901),
83, n. 3.
72 B.C., V, 457-459.
73 C.I.L., VI, 4. ii. p. 3116, Inscription No. 31545.
74 B.C., V, 458.
75 Op cit., pp. 150 ff.

of A.D. 51 as the time that Gallio entered his proconsulship of Achaia.[76]

> Tiberius [Claudius] Caesar Augustus Germanicus, [Pontifex Maximus, in his tribunician] power
> [year 12, acclaimed Emperor for] the 26th time, father of the country, [consul for the 5th time, censor, sends greeting to the city of Delphi.]
> I have for long been zealous for the city of Delphi [and favourable to it from the]
> beginning, and I have always observed the cult of the [Pythian] Apollo, [but with regard to]
> the present stories, and those quarrels of the citizens of which [a report has been made by Lucius]
> Junius Gallio, my friend, and [pro]consul [of Achaea]. . . .[77]

We do not know how long Gallio was proconsul; we do not know for certain whether Paul was brought before him at the beginning or at the end of his term of office; nor do we know when the hearing came in the stay of Paul at Corinth.[78] It is commonly assumed that Gallio was proconsul only one year (A.D. 51), that Paul was brought before him at the beginning of his term, and that the hearing was at the end of Paul's stay in Corinth. From this chain of conjectures, one arrives at the conclusion that A.D. 49-50 marks Paul's arrival. Other dates in the Apostle's life are figured from this point.

Gallio found the climate at Corinth unwholesome for him.[79] He later became a consul.[80] Eventually he became involved in the conspiracy against Nero that ended in Seneca's death. Though he, himself, momentarily escaped, he was the next year forced to commit suicide.[81]

THE HERODS

Herod the Great

By Luke the approaching birth of John the Baptist is dated "in the days of Herod, king of Judea" (1:5). In Matthew the wise men came to Herod in Jerusalem asking for the one born

---

76 A. Deissmann, *Paul*, trans. by W. E. Wilson (New York: Harper and Brothers, 1927, reprinted 1957), pp. 261-286.

77 C. K. Barrett, *The New Testament Background: Selected Documents* (London: S.P.C.K., 1958), pp. 48-49.

78 *B.C.*, V, 463-464.

79 Seneca *Moral Epistles* civ. 1.

80 Pliny *Natural History* xxxi. 33.

81 Tacitus *Annals* xv. 73; Dio Cassius *Roman History* lxii. 25.

king of the Jews (2:1-2). Learning from the scribes that the birth should be in Bethlehem, Herod charged the wise men to find the babe and to return to him (Matt. 2:3-8). When the wise men did not return, Herod slaughtered the male children in Bethlehem that were two years old and under (Matt. 2:16). While Joseph and Mary were in Egypt, Herod died and was replaced in Judea by his son, Archelaus (Matt. 2:22).

Josephus gives a detailed account of Herod in *The Jewish War* and devotes book XIV, all of XV, XVI, and a large part of XVII of the *Antiquities* to Herod. Josephus had for his source in this part of his story Nicholas of Damascus, who had been attached to the court of Herod.

It is beyond our purposes here to give any sort of detailed survey of the career of Herod. He was appointed king in 40 B.C. after holding lesser appointments, but it was not until 37 B.C. that he actually acquired the throne in Jerusalem. He continued as king until his death in 4 B.C. No external source deals with the episode found in Matthew. One recent treatment of Herod[82] and one of the Gospels[83] deny the historicity of the episode. It is known, of course, that Herod slaughtered all rivals. Even within his own family, his favorite wife and several of his sons did not escape once they came under suspicion. Alexander and Aristobulus were executed in 8 B.C., and five days before his own death in 4 B.C. he executed another son, Antipater. The Emperor Augustus is said to have punned following the death of Mariamme's sons, "I would rather be Herod's hog (*hus*) than his son (*huios*)."[84]

Evidence of Herod's extensive building activity has been revealed in excavations at Samaria, Caesarea, Jerusalem, New Testament Jericho, Hebron, Masada, and at Machaerus. Also examples of his coins have been found. These coins have helmets, shields, sacrificial vessels, fruits and the like, but no human figures. Some examples are dated the third year which is perhaps 37 B.C.; some are inscribed in Greek: "Of King Herodes"; others have "Herod the King."[85] An inscription from a decorative column from a ruined temple of the Herodian period found

---

82 S. Sandmel, *Herod; Profile of a Tyrant* (Philadelphia: Lippincott, 1967), p. 262.

83 W. E. Bundy, *Jesus and the First Three Gospels* (Cambridge: Harvard University Press, 1955), p. 34.

84 Macrobius *Saturnalia* ii. 4. 11.

85 Reifenberg, *Israel's History in Coins*, pp. 10, 23, No. 6; J. Meyshan, "The Symbols on the Coinage of Herod the Great and Their Meanings," *PEQ*, XCI (1959), 109-120; Meshorer, *op. cit.*, pp. 64-65.

in Si‘a in the last century honored Herod.[86] Yadin found a potsherd with the inscription, "To King Herod of Judea," in his excavation at Masada.[87]

Archelaus

Only Matthew in the New Testament notices the rule of Archelaus. When Joseph heard that Archelaus reigned over Judea in place of his father Herod, he was afraid to go there. Consequently, he withdrew into Galilee and lived in Nazareth (Matt. 2:22-23).

Archelaus' rule over Judea is surveyed by Josephus. Son of Malthace and an elder brother to Antipas, Archelaus was reared in Rome. He was, at the age of eighteen, following Herod's death (4 B.C.), made ethnarch by Augustus over the territory of Judea, Samaria, and Idumea with the promise of the title of king should he prove worthy of it.[88] This decision grew out of a contest of the will of Herod between Antipas and Archelaus.[89] The two appealed to Rome while a third deputation from the Jewish people requested that no descendant of Herod be appointed as king.

Archelaus built a reputation for being violent and tyrannical.[90] He offended the Jews by his marriage to the twice previously married Glaphyra, wife of his half-brother Alexander, who already had children. Archelaus, himself, divorced his own wife Mariamme prior to this marriage.[91] He at first replaced Joezer in the high priesthood with Eleazar and then later removed Eleazar and appointed Jesus, son of Seë. Archelaus' building activities included restoration of the palace at Jericho, building an aqueduct to water palm groves in the plain north of Jericho, and building a city which he named Archelaïs to honor himself.[92]

After a rule of nine years, the emperor conceded to an accusation made by the Jews and Samaritans jointly, summoned Archelaus to Rome, deposed him, and banished him to Vienna in Gaul in A.D. 6.[93] Strabo remarks about the affair, "one of them

---

86 E. Schürer, "Epigraphische Beiträge zur Geschichte der Herodäer," *ZWT*, XVI (1873), 252-253.

87 *Masada* (New York: Random House, 1966), p. 189.

88 *Ant.* xvii. 11. 4 (317); *War* ii. 6. 3 (93).

89 Josephus *War* i. 32. 7 (646); 33. 7 (664).

90 Josephus *Ant.* xvii. 13. 2 (342); *War* ii. 7. 3 (111).

91 Josephus *Ant.* xvii. 13. 1, 4 (341, 349 f.); *War* ii. 7. 4 (114).

92 Josephus *Ant.* xvii. 13. 1 (340).

93 *Ibid.*, 2-3 (342 ff.); *War* ii. 7. 3 (111); cf. Dio Cassius *Roman History* lv. 27. 6.

spent the rest of his life in exile, having taken up his abode
among the Allobrogian Gauls. . . ."[94]

Coins of Archelaus' period sometimes carry the inscription
"Herod," sometimes the title "Ethnarch," and sometimes either
"Ethnarch Herod" or "of Ethnarch Herod." They tend to be
found in the region of Jerusalem or Jericho but a number of his
coins were found at Masada.[95]

Antipas

Luke dates the appearance of John the Baptist by a series of
rulers which includes "Herod . . . tetrarch of Galilee." (Luke 3:1).
It was he who imprisoned John and later killed him for his denunciation of the marriage of Antipas with Herodias (Matt. 14:
1 ff.; Mark 6:14 ff.; Luke 3:19). He is called "king" (*basileus*) by
Mark (6:14; 6:22 ff.) and by Matthew (14:9). Later when
rumors of the success of the ministry of Jesus came to him, re-
morse of conscience caused him to think that John was risen from
the dead. Aware of his danger, Jesus withdrew from his territory
into that of Philip (Matt. 14:13; Mark 6:14; Luke 9:7-9).

At another time, when Jesus heard that Antipas desired to
kill him, Jesus referred to him as "the fox" (Luke 13:31-32).
Yet again Jesus warned of the "leaven of Herod" (Mark 8:15;
other texts read "Herodians"). At one point the wife of Herod's
steward ministered to Jesus (Luke 8:3). At the trial of Jesus,
Pilate sent Jesus to Herod, who had wished to see him for some
time (Luke 23:7-15; cf. Acts 4:27). Still later one of the teach-
ers at Antioch had been a member of the court of Herod the
tetrarch (Acts 13:1).

The career of Antipas, including his forty-two year reign, is
traced out by Josephus. Like Archelaus, Antipas was a son of
Malthace. Though he contested the will of Herod, he ultimately received Galilee and Perea — two areas separated from
each other — and wore the title "tetrarch." He built his capital on
the shores of Galilee in A.D. 22, named it after Tiberius the emperor, and then populated it with Gentiles.[96] He also rebuilt
Sepphoris.[97]

The first marriage of Antipas was to a daughter of Aretas, the

94 *Geography* xvi. 2. 46.
95 Reifenberg, *Ancient Jewish Coins*, pp. 20, 45-46, Nos. 53-57. Meshorer, *op. cit.*, pp. 69 ff. J. Meyshan, *Essays in Jewish Numismatics* (Tel
Aviv: Israel Numismatic Society, 1968), pp. 56-60, 99-103.

king of the Nabateans. But after falling in love with Herodias, his brother Philip's wife, he planned to divorce the daughter of Aretas; however, she learned of the affair and fled to her father before he could act. Following the arrest of John the Baptist, John was imprisoned at Machaerus.[98] Josephus said that Herod executed him for fear of a rebellion. Ultimately in A.D. 36 Aretas defeated Antipas in retaliation for the slight given his daughter.[99] Stimulated by Herodias, Antipas later went to Rome to request of Gaius elevation to the title of "king." Agrippa, however, brought charges against him, and he was banished to Lugdunum in Gaul.[100] Josephus elsewhere reports that he died in Spain.[101]

Some coins minted in Antipas' territory carry the inscription, "Of Herod the tetrarch."[102] Inscriptions of "Herod the tetrarch" have been discovered on the island of Cos[103] and on the island of Delos,[104] but nothing more is known of his connection with these places.[105]

Herodias

Herodias was the cause of John the Baptist's rebuke of Herod Antipas which rebuke cost John his freedom and his life. Since she had previously been married to his brother Philip and had borne him a child, John insisted that Antipas' marriage to her was not lawful. John was imprisoned and Herodias vented her wrath by stimulating her daughter to ask for John's head on a platter. When Antipas complied with the request, the daughter brought the head to Herodias (Matt. 14:1-12; Mark 6:17-28; Luke 3:19).

Herodias, a daugher of Aristobulus, was a granddaughter of Herod the Great and a sister of Herod of Chalcis, Agrippa I,

---

96 *Ant.* xviii. 2. 3 (36); the career of Antipas has been recently surveyed by F. F. Bruce, "Herod Antipas, tetrarch of Galilee and Peraea," *The Annual of Leeds University Oriental Society,* V (1966), 6-23.

97 Josephus *Ant.* xviii. 2. 1 (27).

98 *Ibid.,* 5. 2 (119).

99 *Ibid.*

100 *Ibid.,* 7. 2 (245 ff.).

101 *War* ii. 9. 6 (183).

102 Reifenberg, *Ancient Jewish Coins,* pp. 19, 44-45, Nos. 45-52; *Israel's History in Coins,* pp. 11, 25, No. 10; Meshorer, *op. cit.,* p. 75; Meyshan, *Essays in Jewish Numismatics,* pp. 56-57, 60.

103 *C.I.G.* 2502.

104 Th. Homolle, "Dedicaces Dellennes," *Bulletin de correspondence Hellenique,* III (1879), 365-367.

105 Schürer, *History of the Jewish People,* I. 2. 17-18.

and the younger Aristobulus.[106] Josephus tells of her marriage to Herod, son of Herod the Great by Mariamme, daughter of Simon the high priest. To him she bore a daughter, Salome, who later married Philip the tetrarch.[107] When on a trip to Rome, Antipas visited his half-brother and persuaded Herodias to marry him on condition that he rid himself of his present wife, the daughter of Aretas IV, king of the Nabateans. The Nabatean princess learned of the affair, outwitted him, and on a pretext returned to her father.[108]

Josephus recounts the imprisonment and death of John the Baptist but does not mention the part played in it by Herodias.[109] Still later, in A.D. 41, when Agrippa I was elevated to kingship by Gaius, Herodias out of jealousy stimulated her husband to request a like rank. When his effort ended in failure and banishment, she, despite an option to do otherwise, accompanied him into Spain in his disgrace[110] saying, "It is not right when I have shared in his prosperity that I should abandon him when he has been brought to this pass."[111]

Philip, Husband of Herodias

Yet another Herod, named Philip in Mark (6:17) and Matthew (14:3; but omitted in Codex Bezae and the Latin versions), was the husband of Herodias prior to her marriage to Antipas. Luke relates the episode (3:19), but the best manuscripts omit the name Philip. It was for taking his half-brother's wife that John the Baptist denounced Antipas.

Details of the complicated intermarriages of the Herod family are given by Josephus, and this sordid affair is no exception. To this member of the family, however, he gives merely the name "Herod":

> Herodias was married to Herod, the son of Herod the Great by Mariamme, daughter of Simon the high priest. They had a daughter Salome, after whose birth Herodias, taking it into her head to flout the way of our fathers, married Herod, her husband's brother by the same father, who was tetrarch of Galilee; to do this she parted from a living husband.[112]

---

106 Josephus *Ant.* xviii. 5. 4 (136).
107 *Ibid.*
108 *Ibid.*, 5. 1 (109-111).
109 *Ibid.* (116-119).
110 Josephus *War* ii. 9. 6 (181-183); cf. *Ant.* xviii. 7. 1 f. (240 ff.).
111 Josephus *Ant.* xviii. 7. 2 (254).
112 *Ibid.*, 5. 4 (136).

Elsewhere Josephus tells of the meeting of the pair and of their plotting marriage when Antipas should dispose of his current wife, the daughter of Aretas IV. This episode took place as Antipas was starting out for Rome and on that occasion lodged with his half-brother Herod.[113]

In view of the facts that outside the Gospels another Herod named Philip is unknown and that Philip the tetrarch is known to have married Salome, Herodias' daughter, it is widely assumed that a confusion of names has taken place in the Gospels. With varying degrees of dogmatism it is asserted that it is unlikely that two half-brothers would have the same name. While it may be unlikely, in an enigmatic family like the Herods, it is not impossible that there were two Philips. Outside the Gospels there really is no evidence either for or against the proposition.

Philip

Luke dates the appearance of John the Baptist by a group of rulers among whom is "Philip tetrarch of the region of Ituraea and Trachonitis" (Luke 3:1).

Though he states the area differently in different passages, from Josephus it is learned that at the death of Herod in 4 B.C., Batanea, Trachonitis, Auranitis, Gaulanitis, and Paneas were assigned to his son Philip, son of Cleopatra of Jerusalem, with the title of tetrarch.[114] Philip was married to Salome, daughter of Herodias. He rebuilt Paneas and renamed it Caesarea Philippi; he also rebuilt Bethsaida where the Jordan flows into Galilee and named it Julias.[115] Philip died in A.D. 34 after a rule of thirty-seven years.

Some coins minted in his reign have been found which carry an inscription, "Philip the Tetrarch."[116] He is the first Jewish ruler to use the effigy of the Roman emperor on his coins. A head of Augustus appears on a coin of A.D. 1-2.[117] One coin of his has been found in an excavation of Curium in Cyprus.[118]

---

113 *Ibid.*, 5. 1 (109-110).
114 *Ibid.*, xvii. 1. 3 (21); 8. 1 (189); 11. 4 (319); xviii. 4. 6 (106); *War* ii. 6. 3 (95).
115 Josephus *Ant.* xviii. 2. 1 (28); *War* ii. 9. 1 (168).
116 Reifenberg, *Ancient Jewish Coins*, Nos. 37-44; Meshorer, *op. cit.*, pp. 76-77; Meyshan, *Essays in Jewish Numismatics*, p. 59.
117 Reifenberg, *Israel's History in Coins*, pp. 10, 24, No. 8.
118 D. H. Cox, *Coins from the Excavations at Curium 1932-1953* (Numismatic Notes and Monographs, No. 145; New York: The American Numismatic Society, 1959), p. 25.

A Nabatean text found at Si^c mentions the erection of a statue "in the year 33 of our Lord Philip"; that is, in A.D. 29/30.[119]

Josephus praises him:

> In his conduct of the government he showed a moderate and easy-going disposition. Indeed, he spent all his time in the territory subject to him. When he went on circuit he had only a few select companions. The throne on which he sat when he gave judgment accompanied him wherever he went. And so, whenever anyone appealed to him for redress along the route, at once without a moment's delay the throne was set up wherever it might be. He took his seat and gave the case hearing. He fixed penalties for those who were convicted and released those who had been unjustly accused. He died in Julias. His body was carried to the tomb that he himself had erected before he died and there was a costly funeral.[120]

Agrippa I

Agrippa I, called by the family name "Herod the king," in Jerusalem put James to death with the sword and arrested Peter until the Passover should be past. His aims against Peter were frustrated by Peter's deliverance from prison in the night (Acts 12:1-13). Herod proceeded to execute the sentries who had not succeeded in safely guarding Peter (Acts 12:19).

Herod spent time at Caesarea. There the people of Tyre and Sidon called upon him asking for peace through the king's chamberlain, Blastus, since their country was dependent upon his for food. On an appointed day Herod put on his royal robes, took his seat upon the throne, and made an oration to them. The people shouted, "The voice of a god and not the voice of man!" An angel of the Lord smote Herod because he did not give God the glory, and he was eaten with worms and died (Acts 12:20-23).

Agrippa I, a grandson of Herod I, was a son of Aristobulus, son of Herod's wife, Mariamme, the Maccabean princess. Aristobulus was executed by Herod in 7 B.C., and Agrippa was sent to Rome for education where he succeeded in getting himself deeply in debt. Eventually he was given the former tetrarchy of Philip with the title of "king" by Caligula in A.D. 37. As he

---

119 E. Littmann, *Semitic Inscriptions*, Publications of the Princeton University Archaeological Expeditions to Syria in 1904-1905 and 1909, Division IV (Leyden: E. J. Brill, 1914), p. 78, No. 101.

120 *Ant.* xviii. 4. 6 (107-108).

proceeded to Palestine, his stop in Alexandria set off anti-Jewish riots which are surveyed by Philo.[121] Once in his territory Agrippa was able to gain favor in the eyes of the Jews. Galilee and Perea were added to his territory in A.D. 39 when Antipas was exiled, and Judea and Samaria were gained by a grant from Claudius in A.D. 41. It was he who persuaded Caligula to rescind his order that his image be put in the temple. Later he, despite his Edomite ancestry, was acknowledged by the Jews on an occasion of the public reading of Deuteronomy 17:15 with the cry: "Be of good cheer, Agrippa! You are truly our brother."[122] He lived in Jerusalem rather than in Caesarea. When his death came in A.D. 44, he was sincerely mourned by the Jews. Since his son Agrippa II was judged under age to enjoy full rule, Judea was again put under procurators.

The book of Acts is the only source of information on the death of James, but Josephus has an account of the death of Agrippa to which Eusebius was glad to appeal as a confirmation of Acts (Eusebius in quoting the passage changes "owl" to "angel"[123]) but which differs in some details from that of Acts.

> After the completion of the third year of his reign over the whole of Judaea, Agrippa came to the city of Caesarea, which had previously been called Strato's Tower. Here he celebrated spectacles in honour of Caesar, knowing that these had been instituted as a kind of festival on behalf of Caesar's well-being. For this occasion there were gathered a large number of men who held office or had advanced to some rank in the kingdom. On the second day of the spectacles, clad in a garment woven completely of silver so that its texture was indeed wondrous, he entered the theater at daybreak. There the silver, illumined by the touch of the first rays of the sun, was wondrously radiant and by its glitter inspired fear and awe in those who gazed intently upon it. Straightway his flatterers raised their voices from various directions — though hardly for his good — addressing him as a god. "May you be propitious to us," they added, "and if we have hitherto feared you as a man, yet henceforth we agree that you are more than mortal in your being." The king did not rebuke them nor did he reject their flattery as impious. But shortly thereafter he looked up and saw an owl perched on a rope over his head. At once, recognizing this as a harbinger of woes just as it had once been of good tidings, he felt a stab of pain in his heart. He was also gripped in his stomach by an ache that he felt everywhere at

121 *Against Flaccus* and *Embassy to Gaius.*
122 *M. Sota* 7. 8.
123 *H.E.* ii. 10. 6.

once and that was intense from the start . . . Exhausted after five straight days by the pain in his abdomen, he departed this life in the fifty-fourth year of his life and the seventh of his reign.[124]

Each of these accounts has independent details though agreeing in others. The writer of Acts and Josephus agree that the event took place in Caesarea, that Herod made a speech while royally clad, and that there was a flattering shout and a sudden death. Acts mentions Blastus, the quarrel with Tyre and Sidon, and worms as the cause of death — all of which Josephus omits. Josephus mentions the feast in honor of Caesar, the silver robe, and the owl as an omen of death with other details which Acts does not give. The relationship of Luke to Josephus is a debated question. It is possible to argue that these are two independent accounts of the same event. The occasion of Herod's speech is one point at issue in the discussion. Josephus does not say too much about Herod's difficulties with his heathen subjects though he does mention that they rejoiced at his death.[125] It is not impossible that the settling of a quarrel with them should fall upon the day of festival. Since this event happened in the Jewish world and no doubt was widely known, Luke would independently have had as free access to sources of information as would Josephus.

A coin from Caesarea, dated A.D. 44-45, has the head of Agrippa and the inscription: "The Great King Agrippa, Friend of the Caesar."[126] Agrippa is the first Jewish ruler to strike his own head on his coins. A basalt fragment with a Nabataean inscription found in Si[c] in the area of Batanaea and Auranitis (now in the art museum at Princeton, New Jersey) reads, "Agrippas the king." It cannot be known whether the king in question is Agrippa I or his son Agrippa II.[127]

Drusilla

A Jewess, Drusilla, wife of Felix, in company with her husband heard Paul during his imprisonment in Caesarea as Paul reasoned of justice, self-control, and future judgment (Acts 24: 24).

---

124 Josephus *Ant.* xix. 8. 2 (343 ff.).
125 *Ibid.*, 9. 1 (355 ff.).
126 Reifenberg, *Israel's History in Coins*, p. 26, No. 12; Meyshan, *Essays in Jewish Numismatics*, pp. 105-115.
127 Littmann, *op. cit.*, IV, 81, No. 102.

Drusilla, a daughter of Agrippa I and a sister of Agrippa II and Bernice,[128] was six years old at the time of the death of her father.[129] Epiphanes of Commagene to whom she was betrothed by her father refused to convert to the Jews' religion and so Drusilla was given in marriage to Azizus, king of Emesa.[130] Felix, by the aid of a magician, Simon of Cyprus, won her from her husband and she bore him a son named Agrippa.[131] She is doubtless to be included among the three queens to whom Suetonius said Felix was married.[132] She and her son disappeared at the time of the eruption of Vesuvius.

Agrippa II

When Agrippa (accompanied by Bernice), upon a visit to Caesarea to welcome Festus, was made acquainted with the problem of the prisoner Paul, he expressed a desire to hear him (Acts 25:13-22). A formal audience was granted and Agrippa gave Paul permission to speak (Acts 25:23; 26:1). Paul flattered the king by reminding him of his knowledge of customs and controversies of the Jews and then told the story of his own life, stressing his obedience to the heavenly vision. When Paul ended with a direct appeal to Agrippa's belief in the prophets, Agrippa turned aside the appeal with: "In a short time you think to make me a Christian!" (Acts 26:2-29). But after the hearing, Agrippa expressed a conviction of Paul's innocence and the opinion that he could have been released had he not already appealed to Caesar (Acts 26:30-32).

The book of Acts is our only source of information on this interview; Agrippa's career, however, came to the attention of both Josephus[133] and of certain Roman writers.

Trained at Rome,[134] Agrippa II (son of Agrippa I and the brother of Bernice and Drusilla) was appointed to the government of Chalcis in A.D. 48 by Claudius. In A.D. 54 he traded Chalcis for the tetrarchy of Philip and other territories.

Tongues whispered scandals concerning his relationship to his sister.[135] A controversy between him and the priests in Je-

---

128 Josephus *Ant.* xviii. 5. 4 (132).
129 *Ibid.*, xix. 9. 1 (354).
130 *Ibid.*, xx. 7. 1 (139).
131 *Ibid.*, 7. 2 (141-144).
132 *Claudius* 28.
133 *Ant.* xx; *War* ii. 16. 4 ff. (345 ff.), *et passim.*
134 Josephus *Ant.* xix. 9. 2 (360).
135 *Ibid.*, xx. 7. 3 (145); Juvenal *Satire* vi. 156-160.

rusalem over a wall which cut off his view of proceedings in the temple when he was visiting there was, despite the support he had from Festus, appealed to Caesar and the wall remained in its place.[136] In the wars of A.D. 66 to 70 Agrippa sided with the Romans. After the war he was confirmed in the possession of his kingdom.[137] He later wrote letters to Josephus and praised him for his *History of the Jews,* and he bought a copy of it.[138] He perhaps lived until A.D. 100 as is attested by Justus of Tiberias.[139]

Three portrait coins of Agrippa, showing him at different stages in life, are known. The first, found at Caesarea Philippi and dated in the year 5 (i.e., A.D. 60), has his youthful likeness and the inscription, "of King Agrippa."[140] A second, found at Paneas is dated in the year 8 (A.D. 58) when he was about thirty-one, and the third is dated in the year 10 (A.D. 64) when he was about thirty-three.[141] As has been suggested above, it cannot be known whether the Nabataean inscription from Si[c] deals with Agrippa II or with Agrippa I.

Bernice

While Paul was in prison in Caesarea, Bernice came with King Agrippa to welcome the newly arrived Festus. She sat in the audience hall with Agrippa and heard Paul deliver his defense. In this context in association with Agrippa her name appears three times in the narrative (Acts 25:13, 23; 26:30).

Bernice was the daughter of Agrippa I and was sister of Agrippa II and Drusilla. At the time of her father's death she was sixteen and already twice married: first to Marcus, son of Alexander an official of Alexandria, and second to Herod her uncle who was king of Chalcis.[142] To the latter she bore two sons.[143] After the death of her uncle-husband in A.D. 48, she

---

136 Josephus *Ant.* xx. 8. 11 (189 ff.).
137 Schürer, *History of the Jewish People,* I. 2, 201-203.
138 Josephus *Life* 65 (361 f.); *Against Apion* i. 9 (47-51).
139 Schürer, *op. cit.,* 205.
140 Reifenberg, *Ancient Jewish Coins,* Nos. 74, 75; cf. *Israel's History in Coins,* p. 28, No. 17. The dating is questioned by J. Meyshan; see the next note.
141 J. Meyshan, "An Unpublished Coin of Agrippa II," *Israel Numismatic Bulletin,* I (1962), 8-9; for other Agrippa II coins, cf. Meshorer, *op. cit.,* pp. 141-153, and H. Seyrig, "Sur quelques ères Syriennes," *Revue Numismatique,* VI, n.s. (1964), 55-65.
142 Josephus *Ant.* xix. 9. 1 (354).
143 *Ibid.,* xx. 5. 2 (104).

became a member of her brother's household, but rumors arose of illicit relations between the two. To quiet these, she married Polemo, king of Cilicia, who consented to circumcision for the sake of the marriage. In a short time she had returned to her brother's household.[144] Even the Roman satirist, Juvenal, tittered about her and the ring her brother gave her, for in a list he mentions

> a diamond of great renown, made precious by the finger of Berenice. It was given as a present long ago by the barbarian Agrippa to his incestuous sister, in that country where kings celebrate festal sabbaths with bare feet, and where a long established clemency suffers pigs to attain old age.[145]

Not beyond the performance of religious acts, Bernice is reported once in A.D. 66 to have been in Jerusalem to fulfill a Nazarite vow.[146]

During the Jewish war, when Agrippa took the oath of allegiance to Vespasian, Bernice was able to charm Titus, who himself is reputed to have been rather profligate. The widespread rumors about the two led some to interpret his trip to Syria to rejoin his father in A.D. 69 following the death of Galba to be a trip on her account.[147] Later, when Bernice came to Rome with her brother in A.D. 75, she lived with Titus in the palace as though married to him. He allegedly promised her marriage,[148] and rivals were punished,[149] but she was eventually sent away.[150] Despite the fact that she again came to Rome after Titus was emperor, she was no longer able to bewitch him.[151]

Bernice is remembered in an inscription from Athens set up by the council and the people there.[152] She is also mentioned along with her brother in a Latin inscription from the Forum in Beirut (discovered in 1927 and now at the Beirut museum) which is restored to read: "Queen Berenice daughter of the great King Agrippa and King Agrippa her brother adorned with

---

144 *Ibid.*, 7. 3 (145).
145 *Satire* vi. 155-160.
146 Josephus *War* ii. 15. 1 (313).
147 Tacitus *Histories* ii. 2.
148 Suetonius *Titus* 7.
149 Schürer, *op. cit.*, 203, n. 38.
150 Dio Cassius *Roman History* lxv. 15. 3-4.
151 *Ibid.*, lxvi. 18. 1.
152 *C.I.G.*, No. 361; *C.I.A.*, iii. 1, No. 556; text also in Schürer, *op. cit.*, 204, n. 39.

marbles and columns the building which their ancestor King
Herod had made, after it had fallen into decay through age."[153]

LESSER JEWISH FIGURES

The High Priests

The term "high priest" is applied in the New Testament to
Annas, Caiaphas, Ananias, and Sceva. The public appearance
of John the Baptist is synchronized with the high priesthood of
Annas and Caiaphas (Luke 3:1-2). Later, Jesus was tried before
both of these figures. Still later Peter and John are arraigned
before "Annas the high priest and Caiaphas and John and Alexander, and all who were of the high-priestly family" (Acts 4:
6). Upon his visit to Jerusalem, Paul was arraigned before Ananias, and the latter was denounced by Paul after he had
commanded that Paul be struck (Acts 23:1 ff.). Shortly thereafter Ananias made a trip to Caesarea with a party to present
complaints against Paul before Felix (Acts 24:1). In contrast
to these officiating figures, in Ephesus "seven sons of a Jewish
high priest named Sceva" unsuccessfully undertook an exorcism
in the name of the Lord Jesus (Acts 19:14).

The vicissitudes of the high priesthood in the New Testament
period can be traced from Josephus.[154] Though the office was
traditionally hereditary and for life, high priests were made
and unmade by whim of the ruling officials in the first century.

Annas was made high priest by Quirinius in A.D. 6, but was
deposed by Valerius Gratus in A.D. 14.[155] He was therefore only
ex-high priest at the time episodes related about him in the
New Testament took place, though the book does not mention
this feature.

Caiaphas was appointed by Valerius Gratus (A.D. 15-26) and
then later was deposed by Vitellius, who was governor of Syria
contemporary with Pontius Pilate.[156]

Ananias, son of Nedebaeos, was appointed by Herod, king of
Chalcis, in A.D. 48.[157] He was a Sadducee and was of evil tem-
per and character according to Josephus. He was eventually
murdered by the insurgents.[158]

153 Stewart Perowne, *The Later Herods* (New York-Nashville: Abingdon Press, 1958), Figs. 27, 28.
154 *Ant.* xviii. 2. 1-2 (26 ff.).
155 *Ibid.*; xx. 9. 1 (203).
156 Josephus *Ant.* xviii. 2. 2 (35); 4. 3 (95).
157 Josephus *Ant.* xx. 5. 2 (103).
158 *Ibid.*, 6. 2 (131); xx. 9. 2-4 (204 ff.); *War* ii. 12. 6 (243); ii.
17. 9 (441 f.).

Of John and Alexander, who belonged to the priestly family, we know nothing more. Codex Bezae has "Jonathan" here. There was a high priest by this name who was the son of Ananus and who was appointed by Vitellius in A.D. 36 in succession to Caiaphas but who was soon removed from office.[159] This character was murdered by the Partisans whom Josephus calls the Assassins.[160] The question which Codex Bezae raises would be whether Bezae preserves the original meaning or has a correction due to knowledge of this man.

Schürer sets forth the idea that both in Josephus and in Acts the term, "high priest," includes the man in office, those who had previously held office, and finally members of the privileged families from whom the actual priests were chosen.[161]

Gamaliel

In Acts, Gamaliel presents a defense for the Apostles in which he refers to the movements of Theudas and Judas that had come to naught. The implication is that the Christian movement would experience a similar fate if let alone and if it be from men rather than from God. Gamaliel is called a Pharisee, a member of the council, a teacher of the law held in honor by all the people (Acts 5:33-39). In his own defense at a later time Paul claims to have been trained at Gamaliel's feet in Jerusalem and to have been educated according to the strict law of the fathers (Acts 22:3).

Not a great deal can be known about Gamaliel. Josephus mentions a man living in A.D. 60-70 who was Simon the son of Gamaliel, from an illustrious family in Jerusalem, a Pharisee.[162] This would make it likely that the father was living at the time represented in Acts. Gamaliel appears in the Mishna as "Gamaliel the Elder." One needs to distinguish him from Gamaliel the second. He was, according to tradition, the first to wear the name Rabban.[163] His sayings in the Mishna tend to alter the Sabbath law and the law of divorce in the interest of convenience and justice.[164] That he was held in honor is evidenced by the story of how a particular year was only provisionally

---

159 Josephus Ant. xviii. 4. 3 (95); 5. 3 (123).
160 Ant. xx. 8. 5 (163).
161 History of the Jewish People, II. 1, 204.
162 Life 38 (190-191).
163 G. F. Moore, Judaism (Cambridge: Harvard University Press, 1927), III, 16.
164 M. Rosh Ha-Shanah 2. 5; Yebamoth 16. 7.

known as leap-year until he gave his approval.[165] It is also shown by the saying, "When Rabban Gamaliel the Elder died, the glory of the Law ceased and purity and abstinence died."[166] One further saying said to be his is: "Provide thyself with a teacher and remove thyself from doubt, and tithe not overmuch by guesswork."[167]

All of these passages do not throw much light on the points raised by Acts. It is not elsewhere stated that he taught publicly. Paul makes no allusion to this training in his epistles. There is considerable contrast in Gamaliel's attitude toward the Christians as manifested in his speech, and that of Paul as a persecutor. This has led some to declare that Paul could not have been his pupil; others reply that the pupil does not always follow the teacher.

Theudas

In the speech of Gamaliel (Acts 5:36) Theudas is represented as having given himself out to be someone and as being joined by about four hundred men. He was slain, and his followers were dispersed.

Josephus knows of one Theudas who caused a rebellion:

> During the period when Fadus was procurator of Judaea, a certain impostor named Theudas persuaded the majority of the masses to take up their possessions and to follow him to the Jordan River. He stated that he was a prophet and that at his command the river would be parted and would provide them an easy passage. With this talk he deceived many. Fadus, however, did not permit them to reap the fruit of their folly, but sent against them a squadron of cavalry. These fell upon them unexpectedly, slew many of them and took many prisoners. Theudas himself was captured, whereupon they cut off his head and brought it to Jerusalem. These, then are the events that befell the Jews during the time that Cuspius Fadus was procurator.[168]

Eusebius alludes to this incident from Josephus as being a confirmation of Acts.[169] A difficulty which he seems to overlook is that the identification of these men as the same Theudas

---

165 *M. Eduyoth* 7. 7.
166 *M. Sota* 9. 15.
167 *M. Aboth* 1. 16.
168 *Ant.* xx. 5. 1 (97-99).
169 *H.E.* ii. 11. 1.

is an anachronism of twelve years. Gamaliel spoke approximately A.D. 34, but Fadus was procurator about A.D. 44-46. Luke represents Theudas as coming before Judas, yet Judas arose in the days of the census. We assume he alludes to the census of Quirinius since he has mentioned no other. This creates another difficulty in the way of identification of the two. Minor contrasts in the accounts are: Luke mentions a definite number of followers who were dispersed and that Theudas claimed to be "somebody"; Josephus alludes to a "great number" of followers, some of whom were slain and many of whom were taken alive, and states that he claimed to be a "prophet." The alternatives seem to narrow down to these two: either the writers have in mind two different characters, or one of them is in error. We have no other evidence for two men of the same name at this time. Conservative scholars have asserted its possibility on the basis of the difficulty of positive identification and on the evidence that there were many uprisings in this general period,[170] providing possibility that another Theudas may have led one of them.[171]

Judas

Gamaliel states that after Theudas, Judas the Galilean arose in the days of the census and drew away some of the people after him. He also perished and the people who followed him were scattered (Acts 5:37).

Josephus refers to a Judas, who brought a revolt in the days of Quirinius, despite the fact that the high priest had previously persuaded the people to accept taxation peaceably.

> But a certain Judas, a Gaulanite from a city named Gamala who had enlisted the aid of Saddok, a Pharisee, threw himself into the cause of rebellion. They said that the assessment carried with it a status amounting to downright slavery, no less, and appealed to the nation to make a bid for independence. They urged that in case of success the Jews would have laid the foundation of prosperity, while if they failed to obtain any such boon, they would win honour and renown for their lofty aim; and that Heaven would be their zealous helper to no lesser end than the furthering of their enterprise until it succeeded. . . .[172]

---

170. Josephus *Ant.* xvii. 10. 4, 8 (269 ff., 285).

171 F. F. Bruce, *The Book of the Acts* (Grand Rapids: Eerdmans, 1956), pp. 124-125.

172 *Ant.* xviii. 1. 1 (4-5).

The revolt proceeded at great height and filled the land with calamities. Josephus later mentions that Tiberius Alexander, the successor to Festus, crucified the sons of Judas of Galilee, who caused the revolt in the days of Quirinius' taxation.[173] He mentions Judas the Galilean as the author of the fourth sect of Jewish philosophy, stating that this sect agreed with the Pharisees in all things, but that:

> . . . they have a passion for liberty that is almost unconquerable, since they are convinced that God alone is their leader and master. They think little of submitting to death in unusual forms and permitting vengeance to fall on kinsmen and friends if only they may avoid calling any man master.[174]

He proceeds to say that it was in the time of Gessius Florus (A.D. 64-66) that the nation began to suffer this madness and that it was provoked by his abuse of authority. It would seem that Josephus is speaking of the same Judas in each of these passages, yet he calls him a Galilean in two of them and a Gaulanite in the other. These two regions are on opposite sides of the Jordan River. Josephus also mentions that Judas is from the city of Gamala, which Pauly-Wissowa locates in Gaulonitis,[175] stating at the same time that the *Talmud* erroneously locates it in Galilee.[176] Contrasts between Josephus' story and that of Acts are: Josephus says nothing of the death of the man; while Gamaliel in Acts says that he was slain, and his followers scattered. Josephus makes him the founder of the fourth sect rather than his movement coming to naught.

THE NABATAEAN KING

Aretas

Paul relates how at Damascus the governor (*ethnarch*) under King Aretas guarded the city of Damascus in order to seize him but that he was let down in a basket through a window in the wall and so escaped (II Cor. 11:32-33). The same episode is related in Acts as a Jewish plot from which he escaped (Acts 9: 23-25).

The Aretas involved in this episode was the Nabataean king,

---

173 *Ibid.*, xx. 5. 2 (102).
174 *Ibid.*, xviii. 1. 6 (23); cf. *War* ii. 8. 1 (118); 17. 8-9 (433); vii. 8. 1 (253).
175 "Gamala," *Pauly-Wissowa*, VII, cols. 689-690.
176 *T. B. ᶜArakin* 32 a-b.

Aretas IV (9 B.C.-A.D. 40), whose center was Petra and who before his accession was named Aeneas.[177] Aretas at first seized power on his own, but was eventually confirmed by Augustus.[178] When Varus had proceeded against the Jews following the death of Herod the Great in 4 B.C., Aretas contributed troops to the force and proceeded to sack the villages of Arous and Soppho.[179]

When dealing with Herod Antipas, we have seen how Josephus relates at length his conflicts with Aretas. Antipas had at first married the daughter of Aretas, but when she learned of his plans to dispose of her in order to marry Herodias, she moved first and on a ruse went to the boundary fortress Machaerus, escaping from there to her father. Aretas used the affair as a pretext of war, and the whole army of Antipas was destroyed. Herod appealed to Tiberius, and the latter ordered Vitellius, governor of Syria, to bring in Aretas dead or alive.[180] Vitellius marched against Aretas, but the death of Tiberius at an opportune moment, A.D. 37, allowed Aretas to go unpunished.[181]

Schürer at the end of the last century reported twenty inscriptions of el Hege dated from Aretas' reign as well as an inscription from Sidon and two from Puteoli.[182] He is called "Charitheth, king of the Nabataeans who loves his people."

More recently there has been discovered an inscription at Khirbet et Tannur which states that a man by the name of Netir'el set up a votive altar during the second year of King Aretas IV, that is, in 7 B.C. for the life of the king and for the life of his wife Huldu.[183] Another inscription found at Madeba, dated in the forty-sixth year of his reign (A.D. 37), the same year as Vitellius' abortive campaign, again describes him as Aretas, king of the Nabataeans, "he who loves his people."[184]

On his coins, distributed throughout his reign, he sometimes appears alone and sometimes together with his queen, who at

---

177 Josephus *Ant.* xvi. 9. 4 (295).
178 *Ibid.*, 10. 9 (353-355).
179 *Ibid.*, xvii. 10. 9 (287); *War* ii. 5. 1 (68).
180 Josephus *Ant.* xviii. 5. 1 (109-115).
181 *Ibid.*, 5. 3 (120-126).
182 *History of the Jewish People*, I. 2. 358, citing J. Euting, *Nabatäische Inschriften aus Arabien* (Berlin: Georg Reimer, 1885), pp. 24-61, Nr. 1-20 and *C.I.S.*, II, 157 f.
183 N. Glueck, *The Other Side of the Jordan* (New Haven: American Schools of Oriental Research, 1940), p. 197; *Deities and Dolphins* (New York: Farrar, Straus and Giroux, 1965), p. 138.
184 *C.I.S.*, II, 196; cf. Jean Starcky, "The Nabataeans: A Historical Sketch," *BA*, XVIII (1955), 98-99.

first was Huldu but later was Shuqaylat.[185] A coin found at Khirbet et Tannur probably has the likeness of Aretas and Shuqaylet.[186] Another was purchased by Glueck at Qasr Rabbah from natives who claimed to have found it there.[187] Still others have come from Petra[188] and from Kerak.[189] Also additional coins beyond those previously known have been found in the Wadi Murabba'at.[190]

The question of how Aretas' authority extended as far north as Damascus in Paul's day is still an unsolved one. The situation is entirely possible, but other positive evidence is lacking. That no coins from Damascus with the imperial insignia for the reigns of Caligula and Claudius have been found has been cited as negative evidence; however, this is not really conclusive. It is not known whether the ethnarch concerned in the episode of Paul is a Jew, an Arab sheik with authority in the city, or a sheik lying in wait outside the city.[191] If Aretas did not actually control Damascus at this time, the last mentioned situation would be a possible one to fill the requirements of the event.[192]

MISCELLANEOUS NEW TESTAMENT NAMES

There are additional coincidences between Biblical names and names discovered in certain grave inscriptions from Jerusalem,[193] but these personages are not likely to be identified with Biblical persons. Even more striking is the discovery of an inscription in the theater at Corinth which informs us that Erastus in appreciation of his appointment as *Aedile* laid the pavement at his own expense.[194] In the Roman letter Paul sends greetings from Erastus, the city treasurer (16:23; cf. Acts 19:22; II Tim. 4:20). The name and city are the same and the identification of the two men has sometimes been espoused, but the offices held by each are different.

---

185 Starcky, *op. cit.*, p. 100.
186 *Ibid.*, p. 96, Fig. 5a; cf. N. Glueck, *Deities and Dolphins*, pp. 11-12, 129.
187 Glueck, *Deities and Dolphins*, pp. 57, 135.
188 *Ibid.*, pp. 130-131.
189 *Ibid.*, p. 135.
190 J. T. Milik and H. Seyrig, "Trésor monétaire de Murabba'at," *Revue Numismatique*, VI, No. 1 (1958), 11-26.
191 Cadbury, *op. cit.*, pp. 19-20.
192 *B.C.*, V, 193-194.
193 E. L. Sukenik, "The Earliest Records of Christianity," *AJA*, LI (1947), 351-365.
194 H. J. Cadbury, "Erastus of Corinth," *JBL*, L (1931), 42-58.

SUMMARY

For the accumulating total of the entire study, this section of the investigation has surveyed seventeen characters for whom there is archaeological material either from inscriptions or coins. Beyond correspondence in chronology and confirmation of official positions held, there is little direct contact with the Biblical material. An additional eleven persons were known to Josephus. This count includes John the Baptist, Jesus, and James, but excludes Theudas for reasons given in the relevant sections.

SUMMARY

A study of this type is destined to be out of date before it is completed. The lamented Paul Lapp reminded us that despite the progress of excavation more of the Middle East is unknown than known.[1] He estimated that only 2 percent of the good archaeological sites in Palestine have been touched, that only rarely is more than 5 percent of a site excavated, and that not more than half of the material from excavated sites has been published. The search continues at a rapid pace and each season lays bare additional ancient remains and enlightens us further, though by no means does each season bring to light new material as directly revelant to Bible characters as that which we have sought in this survey. But with archaeological discovery at its present status we have now finished our extended review of Biblical characters who are also known from archaeological materials. We welcome the studies of both those who would attack the identifications here made and those who would supplement and further support the list here compiled.

Though archaeology has cast a great deal of light on manners and customs of various Biblical periods earlier than the divided kingdom, specific figures of these periods are known to us only from the Bible. That men like Abraham, Moses, David, and Solomon left no traces of themselves by name other than in the Bible may be due in part to the elementary stage of knowledge of the Middle Eastern world but more likely is due to the simple fact that the chief significance of these men is in their role in salvation history. Though they gave birth and shape to the Jewish nation, the surviving literature and the records of that nation are in the Bible itself. The chances seem few that future discovery will greatly change this general picture.

---

1 "Palestine; Known But Mostly Unknown," *BA.,* XXVI (1963), 121-134.

For the later period the situation is different. From the Egyptian sphere of influence the four figures: Shishak, Tirhakah, Necho, and Hophra, are well-attested figures in archaeological sources. The remaining Egyptian king, "So, king of Egypt," who is mentioned by name in the Bible continues to perplex us.

The most abundant material comes from the Assyrians who overran and dominated Palestine through most of the period of the Israelite monarchy. Between the time of the first contact of Assyria with Israel at the Battle of Qarqar until the battle of Carchemish twelve Assyrian kings are known from Assyrian, Babylonian, and classical sources to have reigned. The Old Testament reflects the contacts of six of them with Israel and Judah. They are Tiglath-pileser III, Shalmaneser V, Sargon II, Sennacherib, Esarhaddon, and Ashurbanipal. The names of the less significant figures Adrammelech and Sharezer may possibly also have been identified.

From the near neighbors of Israel — the Moabites and the Arameans — we have found occurrence of the names of five figures. These are Mesha of Moab and four Syrians: Ben-hadad I, Hazael, Ben-hadad II, and Rezin.

Five rulers or officials of the Babylonians: Merodach-baladan, Nebuchadnezzar, Evil-merodach, Nergalsharezer, and Belshazzar, whose activities brought them into contact with Judah, have been found mentioned in Middle Eastern records.

Of the Israelites themselves, out of the nineteen figures who are known to have occupied the throne of Israel — legitimately or otherwise — after the division of the kingdom, the names of seven kings: Omri, Jehu, Jehoash, Jeroboam II, Menahem, Pekah, and Hoshea are found in the records of their neighbors or upon seals. Of the nineteen Judean kings, six kings: Uzziah, Jotham, Ahaz, Hezekiah, Manasseh, and Jehoiachin, are clearly attested. There are also seals of the governor Gedaliah and of the official Jaazaniah making a total of fifteen Israelite figures from the two kingdoms. While the number is small when compared with the total number of persons named in the Old Testament, it is still an impressive figure.

Of the five Persian kings who reigned in the period surveyed in the Old Testament, only Cambyses goes unmentioned in the Bible. The other four: Cyrus, Darius, Xerxes (Ahasuerus), and Artaxerxes are abundantly known. Of figures of lesser rank, Tattenai, Sanballat, Tobiah, Geshem, and Jehohanan have been identified. The total from this period is nine names with one more possible identification — that of Mordecai. On the opposite

side of the picture, sources continue to be wanting to solve the
questions concerning the problematic Darius the Mede.

Looked at from a wider point of view, forty-four Old Testament figures have with reasonable certainty been identified
with figures whose names occur in the various sorts of ancient
records of the Middle East. In most of the instances the archaeological information supplements the Biblical information
rather than dealing directly with the same episodes that the
Old Testament relates. But notable exceptions are to be found
in Shishak's invasion of Palestine, in Mesha's struggle with Israel, in Menahem's tribute, in Ahaz's tribute, in the overthrow
of Pekah and the accession of Hoshea and his tribute to Assyria, in the succession of Hazael to Ben-hadad I and the later
succession of Ben-hadad II, in the capture of Samaria and the
exiling of its people, in Sargon's campaign against Ashdod, in
Sennacherib's invasion of Judah and his later death and the succession of Esarhaddon to the throne, in Nebuchadnezzar's battle at Carchemish, in his capture of Jerusalem in 597 b.c. and in
the fall of Babylon. For each of these Old Testament events there
is both a Biblical and an extra-Biblical account.

In the New Testament area the archaeological discoveries
are fewer because the span of time covered is much less than
that covered by the Old Testament. On the other hand literary
sources make a valuable contribution concerning the characters
though the contribution is seldom in discussion of the episodes
in which these persons are involved in the New Testament.
Authentic relics have not survived. Seventeen New Testament
figures are known from coins or from other types of inscriptions.
These include Augustus Caesar, Tiberius Caesar, Claudius Caesar, Quirinius, Lysanias, Pontius Pilate, Felix, Sergius Paulus,
Gallio, Herod the Great, Archelaus, Herod Antipas, Herod
Philip, Agrippa I, Agrippa II, Bernice, and Aretas VI. An additional eleven figures were known to Josephus, to Mishnaic
sources, or to classical historians where these writers are not
thought to have had New Testament books as one of their
sources of information. Such figures are Festus, Herodias,
Drusilla, Annas, Caiaphas, Ananias, Gamaliel, Judas the Galilean, Jesus, John the Baptist, and James. Whether the allusion
to Jesus in Josephus is authentic or is a Christian interpolation
continues to be debated. Minor later allusions to Christ are
found in Pliny, Tacitus, and Suetonius.

Biblical episodes which are connected with these New Testament characters that are discussed elsewhere in the literary
sources include Herodias' marriage to Herod Agrippa, John the

Baptist's preaching and his death at the hands of Herod Agrippa, Jesus' crucifixion under Pontius Pilate, the death at Caesarea of Herod Agrippa I, the famine under Claudius and his expulsion of Jews from Rome. The major unsolved questions connected with the New Testament figures that we have included in this survey center around the census of Quirinius and around the figure Theudas.

Combining the forty-four figures we have previously considered in the Old Testament with the seventeen of the New Testament for which there is inscriptional evidence, we have accumulated a total of sixty-three persons. And though it is combining things not precisely equal, if the eleven additional figures from the literary sources are added in, the total rests at seventy-four without claiming those identifications that are possible but which remain in the doubtful category.

Surely contemplation of this collection and the data pertinent to these characters increases one's appreciation for understanding of the story told in the Bible. Perhaps the most fitting admonition with which to close the study is one borrowed from the lips of our Lord in an entirely different context: "Go and learn what this means" (Matt. 9:13).

INDEX OF SCRIPTURE REFERENCES

INDEX OF NAMES AND AUTHORS